Catholic
ANSWERS
to
Fundamentalists'
Questions

Philip St. Romain

Revised, Expanded, and Referenced
to the *Catechism of the Catholic Church*

Liguori
LIGUORI, MISSOURI

Imprimi Potest: Thomas D. Picton, C.Ss.R.
Provincial, St. Louis Province, The Redemptorists

Imprimatur: Most Reverend Robert J. Hermann, V.G.
Auxiliary Bishop of St. Louis

Published by Liguori Publications, Liguori, Missouri
www.liguori.org

Library of Congress Cataloging-in-Publication Data

St. Romain, Philip A.
    Catholic answers to fundamentalists' questions : revised, expanded and
referenced to the Catechism of the Catholic Church.—Rev. ed.
        p. cm.
    Includes bibliographical references (p.)
    ISBN-13: 978-0-7648-1341-2 (pbk.)
    1. Catholic Church—Apologetic works—Miscellanea. I. Catholic Church.
Catechismus Ecclesiae Catholicae. II. Title.

BX1752.S73   2005
230'.2—dc22   2005044291

The editor and publisher gratefully acknowledge permission to reprint/
reproduce copyrighted works granted by the publishers/resources listed on
page 87.

Liguori Publications, a nonprofit corporation, is an apostolate of the Redemptorists. To learn more about the Redemptorists, visit *Redemptorists.com*.

Printed in the United States of America
10   6 5 4 3
Revised edition 2005

Contents

To Herman Sensat (1949–85), who turned my mind toward Christ when I was going astray, then helped me appreciate the richness of Catholicism as a way to live and grow. He was a true friend and spiritual brother.

And James Arraj, very fine Catholic theologian, mentor, and friend.

Acknowledgments

The first edition of this book would not have happened without the support, encouragement, and editorial assistance of Roger Marchand, who was then (1983–1984) an editor at Liguori Publications. Roger took what I now recognize to be a merely promising manuscript and helped it become a solid, useful work. Sadly, he has since passed away, but his influence on this and countless other Liguori books lives on.

My current working relationship with Heartland Center for Spirituality in Great Bend, Kansas, affords me time to read, reflect, and write. Without this, I would not have been able to revise this work. Thanks Sister Louise and team! It's great to work with you!

Much of my ministry with Heartland Center involves Internet-related outreach. The discussion forums at www.shalomplace.com have been a good ongoing resource for listening to and dialoguing with fundamentalists. Thanks to all who have participated.

Since the first edition of this book was published twenty years ago, there have been many very fine works on the topic of Catholicism and fundamentalism that have enriched my understanding on this topic. The authors of these works are too many to mention. See the References section at the end of this book for a few examples.

Finally, I wish to acknowledge the ongoing support of my loving wife, Lisa, and our children, Rita, Theresa, and Paul. I know it's not always easy to live with an introverted thinker. Thanks, gang, for your understanding. It was fun to discuss this book with you when the right time came along.

Foreword

The first edition of this book (1984) was precipitated by encounters with anti-Catholic fundamentalist Christians. We lived in Baton Rouge, Louisiana, at the time, and Jimmy Swaggart Ministries was a short distance from our home. Many Catholics were leaving our parish and going to his beautiful new worship center. Swaggart had several publications that were widely circulated, and which misrepresented a number of Catholic beliefs and practices. In addition, this was the golden age of televangelism, with Jim and Tammy Bakker, Jerry Falwell, and Pat Robertson. Fundamentalist Christians were clearly on the offensive and Catholics, it seemed, were often at a loss for how to respond to some of the attacks against our religion. This problem showed up in the workplace, which became a staging ground for proselytizing, and even (most painfully) in many homes, where converts to a fundamentalist Church accused their Catholic family members of not being saved, or of belonging to a religion that the Bible called the "whore of Babylon."

Catholic Answers to Fundamentalists' Questions provided a basic resource for Catholics who were being pressured to account for their beliefs to fundamentalists. The questions and answers attempted to deal with the most common types of topics that came up in discussions with fundamentalists, and the Appendix by Father Pat Kaler provided additional information on the Bible. As it turned out, the book also became a resource used in many other contexts, including the RCIA, high-school religion classes, and even adult education programs. In many cases, it provided a quick refresher course for adult Catholics who, admittedly, didn't always know their faith well enough to respond to fundamentalists.

A lot has happened since that first edition of this book was published, although much remains the same as well. Radio and televangelism is still a potent force and proselytizing still goes on in the workplace and in families. Fundamentalist "Bible Churches" outnumber Catholic and mainline Protestant Churches in Wichita, Kansas, where we now reside and they seem to be growing faster than any other Christian denomination around the U.S., if not the world. Catholic teachings are still being misrepresented, and the Bible is still being used as a weapon to discredit Catholicism. But we also have many resources in Catholicism that we didn't have in 1984: an official Catechism, a stronger Catholic presence on television and radio, numerous books and pamphlets that respond to fundamentalism, and Internet Web sites and discussion groups that allow the encounters to take place in ways that were impossible in 1984. I have learned much from these new developments and resources that will help to strengthen this second edition.

The basic objectives of this work remain the same as the first edition. First, I hope to provide a response to the basic questions and issues that fundamentalists raise about Catholicism. This core of the book remains unchanged, except for the addition of references to the *Catechism of the Catholic Church* and a sharpening of some of the responses. In many ways, then, this present work continues to provide a kind of "mini-Catechism" or overview of the Faith for Catholics. Chapter one, which was originally part of the introduction, deals with the nature and development of fundamentalism. The chapter of the original work on "Human Origins and Destiny" has been split into two separate chapters in the new edition to provide a more in-depth reflection on these topics. Finally, I've added a chapter on how Catholics and fundamentalists can get along better—both in the home, workplace, and in the world. There are many important areas were we stand together and need one another to help promote a more Christian vision in this world. It may well be that a greater emphasis on what we hold in common can lessen the spirit of conflict and judgment that has characterized so many Catholic-fundamentalist discussions. Such is my hope, at least.

1

What Is Biblical Fundamentalism?

The term *fundamentalist* is now used in a general way to describe anyone from any religion who takes a literalist approach to Scripture or religious dogma, and who is somewhat aggressive in their insistence that this is the only correct way to understand things. In this sense, we have come to speak of biblical fundamentalists, Islamic fundamentalists, and even Catholic fundamentalists.

Q. Why use the term *fundamentalist*? Why not use *literalist*?

Originally, the term was used in reference to a conservative movement in evangelical Protestantism at the turn of the twentieth century. Reacting to what they believed to be liberal trends that compromised basic Christian beliefs, scholars from the Moody Bible Institute published a series of small books between 1910–1915 summarizing their disagreements with liberal Protestantism. These books were called *Fundamentals: A Testimony to the Truth*. Christians who agreed with the theology proposed in the *Fundamentals* series came to be known as "fundamentalists." Since that time, the term has become used to describe other groups as well.

Q. Some fundamentalist Christians like to portray themselves as living a kind of basic, pure Christianity similar to that of the early Church. From what you're saying, it sounds like their origins are more recent.

That's correct. Given the broad scope of the Christian tradition, fundamentalism of the sort we see today is a relatively modern phenomenon, tracing to the great evangelical revivals of the nineteenth century in the United States. Of course, the early Christians did believe many of the doctrines promoted by some fundamentalists—and it should be noted that Catholics also agree with many of these biblical principles as well—but there's absolutely no evidence for the existence of early Christian communities that took Scripture so literally and relied on it so exclusively as the fundamentalists. In fact, there weren't even New Testament books available for Christians for many decades following the life of Christ, and these books were not collected as a body of texts (known as the *canon* of Scripture) for several centuries. Instead, the first Christians mostly relied on the teachings of the leaders of the Church for guidance concerning Christian beliefs.

Q. What did the *Fundamentals* series teach?

It is not possible here to provide an in-depth review of these works. The core message, however, affirmed five basic beliefs which they believed liberalism eroded:

1. The *verbal inspiration* of the Bible: that the Bible truly is the Word of God and is to be understood more or less literally, that is, as meaning what it says and saying what it means.
2. The *virgin birth* of Jesus: that his human Father was God, and not Joseph.
3. The *substitutionary atonement* of Jesus: that he died for our sins.
4. The *bodily resurrection* of Jesus: that his physical body was raised from the tomb. This belief also asserts the divinity of Christ.
5. The imminent and visible *Second Coming* of Jesus: that he truly will come at the end of this age to judge the living and the dead.

Q. This doesn't sound so controversial. Don't most Christians believe these five points?

Except for point #1, which we will reflect on more deeply in forthcoming chapters, most Christians do affirm these five points. It should be noted, however, that at the time when the *Fundamentals* were written, "liberal" theologians were calling all of this into question, or at least they were attempting to come to a new understanding of the meaning of these beliefs in light of developments in science and biblical studies. Of course, it is the task of theologians to do this kind of work and very few are or were overly "adventurous" or "liberal" in their speculations, nevertheless many conservative Christians felt that *any* biblical interpretation beyond the strict letter was too much. The response in *Fundamentals* goes to the heart of what they perceived to be the problem: namely, the contextual interpretation of Scripture.

Q. What are some other characteristic beliefs of biblical fundamentalists?

Flowing from their belief in the verbal inspiration of the Bible and its literal inerrancy, they oppose any theological development which they believe compromises the truths of Scripture as they understand it. One common example is their insistence that the theory of evolution conflicts with the Genesis account of Creation and, therefore, cannot be true. Instead, fundamentalists generally support creationism, which is an attempt to show how the Genesis account of Creation can be understood in scientific terms.

The World Congress of Fundamentalists, which met in Edinburgh, Scotland, in 1976, emphasized that *a fundamentalist is a born-again believer in the Lord Jesus Christ who*

1. Maintains an immovable allegiance to the inerrant, infallible, and verbally inspired Bible.
2. Believes that whatever the Bible says is so.
3. Judges all things by the Bible and is judged only by the Bible.
4. Affirms the foundational truths of the historic Christian Faith: The doctrine of the Trinity; the Incarnation, virgin birth, substitutionary atonement, bodily resurrection and glorious ascension, and the Second Coming of the Lord Jesus Christ; the new birth through regeneration by the Holy Spirit; the resurrection of the

saints to life eternal; the resurrection of the ungodly to final judgment and eternal death; the fellowship of the saints, who are the body of Christ.

5. Practices fidelity to that Faith and endeavors to preach it to every creature.

6. Exposes and separates from all ecclesiastical denial of that Faith, compromise with error, and apostasy from the Truth.

7. Earnestly contends for the Faith once delivered.

Q. OK, so that's what they believe. Why not "live and let live"? They can believe what they want and so can we.

That would be ideal, however, fundamentalists are strongly convinced that their way of understanding the Bible is the only correct way, and that anyone who disagrees with them is wrong. They're also convinced that the end times are near and that in the wake of some great cataclysm, those who are not decisively "born-again" will be confined to hell. This urgency motivates them to proselytize anyone who doesn't believe as they do. According to them, salvation depends upon evangelization. Unfortunately, their proactive approach often causes conflicts with those who either disagree with their fundamental principles or who do not want to be proselytized by them at all. Without any middle ground, it is usually very difficult to live and let live.

Q. Don't they realize that their views about the Bible are an interpretation just like everyone else's?

By taking the words of the Bible literally, fundamentalists think they are avoiding the pitfalls of interpretation that have challenged and split so many Christian denominations throughout the centuries. Their solution to the problem of disunity in Christendom is to take the Bible as God's unambiguous Word to humanity, laying aside *all* subjective human interpretations which, according to them, compromise the meaning of Scripture and lead to contentiousness and factions. Of course, as you suggest, their "objective" approach to the letter of Scripture is itself "subjective"—an interpretation just like everyone else. For example, they inconsistently translate many passages of Scripture, sometimes advocating a strict literalist approach while other times ignoring or even discounting the face value of the text.

Q. Where can one find examples of biblical fundamentalism? Is there an official denomination?

There are Christian communities that can trace their origins to groups based on the *Fundamentals* series, but in general, biblical fundamentalism cuts across many denominations. Fundamentalism exists wherever one finds the kinds of beliefs and strong proselytizing efforts described above. Most nondenominational "Bible churches" are fundamentalist, as are many communities which claim to be evangelical or Pentecostal.

Q. Most Evangelical or Pentecostal communities consider themselves to be Protestant. Are all Protestants fundamentalists?

While all Protestants accept the Bible as the sole source of revealed truth, with strong emphasis on preaching, only a few denominations advocate the zealous evangelical methodology so typical of fundamentalists. Like Catholicism, most mainline Protestant denominations—for example, Lutheran and Episcopal—have developed a scholarly system of checks and balances to safeguard radical interpretation of the Bible. Therefore, in actuality, relatively few Protestants are fundamentalists in the sense described above, but all fundamentalists claim to be rooted in the Protestant tradition.

Q. Are there Catholic fundamentalists?

Officially, no, there are not. There are probably some Catholics who would go along with the teachings of the *Fundamentals,* but the official doctrines of the Church are at odds with several key directives of biblical fundamentalism—especially its view of biblical inspiration and interpretation. Sometimes the term *Catholic fundamentalist* is used in a wider sense, referring to Catholics who adopt a legalistic and literalist view of Catholic *doctrine*, which is based on Scripture but subject to different interpretive norms. Sometimes labeled "conservative" or even "archconservative," these Catholics typically adhere to mainstream Catholic biblical interpretation, and they rarely advocate the forceful proselytizing tactics that characterize biblical fundamentalists.

2

Catholics and the Bible

Catechism of the Catholic Church (CCC):
76, 78, 80–84, 95, 104, 108–114, 120, 129,
131–133, 138, 140–141, 2653–2654

Q. Why do Catholic bibles contain different books from Protestant bibles?

The number, order, and arrangement of the books in the Christian bible—the so-called "canon" of Scripture—developed during the first several centuries of Christianity. Except for variations in translation, the New Testament canon has always been the same for Catholics and Protestants. However, the Catholic version of the Old Testament contains several books not found in Protestant bibles.

The discrepancy dates all the way back to the eighth century before Christ, a time when certain Jews regarded several Greek books as equally inspired as the rest of the Hebrew Scriptures. These books were standardized in one of the most influential Greek translations of the Old Testament, the *Septuagint*, which, along with other Hebrew versions, was adopted by many early Christians. A few early Christians questioned the authenticity of these "extra" books, opting solely for Hebrew translations of the Old Testament. During the sixteenth century their doubts became one of the rallying cries of the Protestant reformers who felt that the Hebrew collection was somehow more pure. Consequently, they removed them from their liturgies and bibles altogether. Today Protestants refer to these "extra" books as "deuterocanonical," or more commonly, "Apocrypha." Catholics, on the other hand, following saints Ambrose, Augustine, and many others throughout history, continue to recognize the ancient Jewish validity of these books. In response to the Reformers' objections, the Roman Catholic Church finally standardized the Old Testament canon at the Council of Trent (1546) and the First Vatican Council (1870). Due to recent discoveries of ancient scrolls, many modern Christians—Catholic and Protestant—recognize the diverse influence and importance of the *Septuagint* translation of the Bible, but few have altered their Old Testament canon. Fundamentalists categorically deny the importance of these "extra" books.

Q. Why doesn't the Catholic Church make use of the King James Bible? It's been the standard translation for the English-speaking world since the early seventeenth century.

The *KJV* is one of the oldest English translations of the Bible, and its verses, expressed in Elizabethan splendor, are part of our religious vocabulary, particularly Christian hymns. However, since its first distribution in 1611, some five hundred other translations have been published in English.

One obvious justification for these translations is that the English-speaking world has changed; no one speaks seventeenth-century English anymore. Second, as human understanding and science have developed new ways of analyzing history and linguistics, biblical scholars have uncovered countless errors in the old English translations. The *Revised Standard Version* (1952) and the *New Revised Standard Version* (1990) are the most recent correctives to the *KJV.* The *NRSV* and other modern English versions of the Bible (including popular Catholic editions such as the *New American Bible, Jerusalem Bible*, and so forth) attempt to convey as closely as possible the meaning intended by the ancient manuscripts using modern English idioms.

Q. Why do so many Catholic beliefs and practices have little, if any, basis in Scripture?

This question gets at the heart of most of the issues raised by fundamentalists. Christian groups that base themselves solely on the words of Scripture have always been critical of those Roman

Catholic beliefs and practices (*traditions*) that cannot be found explicitly in the Bible. Some fundamentalists label all such "non-scriptural" traditions as non-Christian or even anti-Christian.

Two brief responses suggest themselves at this point. First, sometimes the issue is related to biblical interpretation: often Catholic beliefs are indeed rooted in Scripture, but fundamentalists discount bible-based traditions that do not *exactly* comply with their interpretation. For example, while the Catholic celebration of the Eucharist comes directly from the gospels, nevertheless, fundamentalists do not interpret it with the same sacramental emphasis and, as such, they classify the Catholic version as non-scriptural altogether. Second, Catholics affirm the divine character of both Scripture *and* sacred Tradition: "[They] are bound closely together and communicate one with the other. For both of them, flowing from the same divine wellspring, come together in some fashion to form one thing and move towards the same goal" (*CCC* #80). In other words, Catholics believe that Scripture *and* Tradition should be "honored with equal sentiments of devotion and reverence" (*CCC* #82).

Q. What exactly do you mean by sacred Tradition?

Much of the New Testament records the traditions of the early Church. Saint Paul, in particular, emphasized the importance of tradition, saying: "So then, brothers and sisters, stand firm and *hold fast to the traditions* that you were taught by us, either by word of mouth or by our letter" (2 Thessalonians 2:15, emphasis added).

Sacred Tradition "transmits in its entirety the word of God which has been entrusted to the apostles by Christ the Lord and the holy Spirit; it transmits it to the successors of the apostles so that, enlightened by the Spirit of truth, they may faithfully preserve, expound and disseminate it by their preaching" (Dogmatic Constitution on Divine Revelation, 9). Sacred Tradition embraces both the handing-on *process* of the gospel message, and its *products*; that is, the various forms and ways in which God's Word moves from the apostles to the present age. In other words, Christians, first and foremost, understand God in and through their experience of Jesus as revealed in Scripture. Then, through Scripture, Jesus is brought to life through the succession of church leaders and communities from the apostles to modern times. Examples of basic forms of sacred Tradition include the Bible (viewed as a tangible tool for handing on God's word), the Apostles' Creed, and the primary forms of Christian worship (for example, the liturgy). Traditions typically attacked by fundamentalists as nonbiblical—such as the Assumption of Mary and papal infallibility to name just two—share the same divine source as Scripture, and they are evident through the continuing grace of the Holy Spirit in the Church.

Q. Are Roman Catholics really Bible Christians?

Catholics do not believe Christianity to be a mere "book religion" but a unique relationship between God and those human beings who follow his Son, Jesus Christ. Christianity is the story of the Church, and it is only in this context that the Bible can be properly appreciated. Catholics recognize the Bible to be the authentic written expression of the faith of the early Church. They also believe that the Holy Spirit guides the Church with its interpretation of biblical revelation, unfolding the truth of the gospels over time. Therefore, Catholics rigorously examine Scripture with respect to the lived experience of Jesus in the Church. Catholics are biblical Christians in the sense that they reverence Scripture as inspired by God. Perhaps more than any other denomination, Catholics incorporate Scripture into every facet of their prayer life, including the Mass, Divine Office, music, and so forth. In other words, Catholics do not treat Scripture as a document that is extra-ecclesial (outside the Church). They approach Scripture as a gift from God to the Church—a gift that has its home within the Church—because they believe that Christ came primarily to form a community of believers, not primarily to write a holy book that has its total meaning apart from the faith community.

Q. But we know that only the Bible is the Word of God. Why should anyone believe sacred Tradition is important? On the contrary, the Bible warns against placing mere human traditions above the Word of God!

Sacred Tradition cannot be considered a "mere human tradition" because it has its origin in the Word of God and the faith-response of the same communities that gave us the Bible—the undisputed Word of God. The same Church solemnly declares that "both scripture and tradition must be accepted and honored with equal devotion and reverence" by Catholics (Divine Revelation, 9). The Church is the faith-community that gave birth to the New Testament Scriptures and which affirms the authenticity of both the Old and the New Testaments. The Church is therefore justified in affirming the importance of sacred Tradition as a source of beliefs and practices.

Q. Doesn't the Bible stand on its own authority?

It depends upon what one means by "authority" or "authorship." Is Scripture the Word of God? Yes! Was Scripture written by human hands? Yes! Christians must discern how God spoke through the authors of the Bible.

As works inspired by the Holy Spirit, the writings of the New Testament do indeed claim an authority of their own. That is why they were read and circulated in the early Church, along with the Jewish Scriptures. The critical issue here has to do with authoritative discernment and teaching. Since the earliest days of the Church, the decisions of the apostles have been considered authoritative. Based on their firsthand witness of Christ, they were able to discern the difference between inspired writings (canonical) and uninspired writings (those excluded from the canon). Fundamentalists take a rigid stance on the transmission of God's Word into writing, often ignoring the human climate of the New Testament and refusing to translate the words of the first Church into modern understanding.

Q. But the apostles have died, and, besides, many Catholic beliefs and practices arose after the Apostolic Age. How can these latter traditions be considered sacred?

It is easy to consider Tradition sacred when we venerate it as the Church's way of handing on "God's word which was entrusted to the apostles." The fact that some parts of Tradition emerged later than others does not make them less sacred, because "the tradition that comes from the apostles makes progress in the church, with the help of the holy Spirit" (Divine Revelation, 8). The power of the Spirit and the Word of God do not lessen as time goes on. Indeed, Catholics believe that sacred Tradition makes the Word of God and the power of the Spirit even more manifest as history goes on, for "there is a growth in insight into the realities and words that are being passed on.…As the centuries go by, the church is always advancing towards the plenitude of divine truth, until eventually the words of God are fulfilled in it" (Divine Revelation, 8).

This is not to say that every custom or pious belief that has arisen in the Church is a handing-on of God's Word. There have, in fact, been developments which have obscured the Word of God. But, thanks to the constant guidance of the Holy Spirit, such traditions continue to be filtered and defined by the Church's teaching authority and are not yet part of sacred Tradition.

Q. But doesn't such heavy reliance on tradition render God's Word confusing and impotent?

When we understand tradition for what it is—the passing on of God's Word to each new generation—we see that in actuality Scripture is impotent *without* Tradition. Preaching, for example, is an indispensable form of tradition. Preaching is the Gospel passed on by word of mouth, and throughout the ages preaching has been recorded, studied, and voiced from generation to generation. As Paul tells us in Romans 10, faith comes by hearing and hearing comes from preaching. So faith in God's word clearly comes from the process of sacred Tradition.

Most of the criticisms advanced by fundamentalists against sacred Tradition have to do with *products* of the tradition process that are parascriptural. These are elements, beliefs, and practices that receive little or no explicit mention in Scripture but do not run counter to Scripture. In the category of beliefs, three of the most criticized elements are the Immaculate Conception, the Assumption of Mary into heaven, and papal infallibility. Among practices that pertain to Tradition in varying degrees, the following come under fire: the Mass in its fully developed form, priestly celibacy, male priesthood, the seven sacraments in their fully developed form, and devotion to the saints. The gradual adoption of these forms into Church belief and practice did not indicate a disregard for the Word of God; in its own way, each of them is an aid to passing on that very Word. No belief or practice has any justification independent of the interacting realities we know as Church, Scripture, and Tradition. When it comes to the Word of God and divine revelation, the normative guide for Catholics is Scripture.

> It is clear, therefore, that, in the supremely wise arrangement of God, sacred tradition, sacred scripture and the magisterium of the church are so connected and associated that one of them cannot stand without the others. Working together, each in its own way under the action of the one holy Spirit, they all contribute effectively to the salvation of souls.
>
> *DOGMATIC CONSTITUTION ON DIVINE REVELATION, 10*

Q. Surely Catholic doctrines have changed through the ages. Doesn't this mean that the Catholics have changed the meaning of Scripture to suit their tradition?

Human culture has changed many times in the nearly two thousand years during which Christianity has been handed on. The sacred task of preaching the Gospel to every generation has made it necessary to spell out the unchangeable content of revelation anew in the changeable thought-forms and languages of people in every new era and culture.

In this process of preaching and explaining the Gospel anew, ecumenical councils play a key role. An ecumenical council—from the Greek *Oecumenon* meaning "the whole inhabited world"—is an official meeting by bishops and other ecclesiastical leaders of the world for the purpose of decision-making on matters of faith, morals, worship, and discipline. Ecumenical decisions are considered binding for the entire Church. The most recent ecumenical council, Vatican II, did what the teaching Church has always done: bring forward the unchangeable content of revelation, translating it into thought-forms of people in today's culture. Revelation has not changed, but our understanding of it has indeed changed and deepened. Under the guidance of the Holy Spirit, the Church continues to experience "growth in insight into the realities and words that are being passed on" (Divine Revelation, 8).

Q. If the Catholic Church considers Scripture its normative guide, why does the Catholic leadership discourage Catholics from reading the Bible?

Catholics are encouraged to read the Bible, to study its meaning, to pray with its verses, and to use it as the keystone of faith development. That has been the case for many decades now. Indeed, Vatican Council II states: "...the holy synod forcefully and specifically exhorts all the christian faithful...to learn 'the surpassing knowledge of Jesus Christ' (Philemon 3:8) by frequent reading of the divine scriptures. 'Ignorance of the scriptures is ignorance of Christ'" (Divine Revelation, 25).

During some periods of history, particularly during the early part of the Protestant Reformation, Catholics—the majority of whom were uneducated—were discouraged from reading the Bible and formulating their own interpretation. The idea was to safeguard Scripture and its development in sacred Tradition so as to prevent further schism in the Church. Many bishops feared that if their uneducated people read the Bible privately, they would misinterpret it and twist it "to their own destruction" (2 Peter 3:16). Since most lay Catholics were illiterate, they rightfully offered no resistance, opting instead for the long-standing practice of learning Scripture through preaching. The Protestants, on the other hand, felt that Catholicism exalted tradition at the expense of Scripture. They claimed that such moderation of the laity would only perpetuate an already corrupt interpretation of the Word. Thus, some reformers abandoned all Catholic tradition, encouraging believers to study the Bible alone (*sola Scriptura*). Thankfully in the centuries that followed, Protestants and Catholics have found a middle ground: Protestants appreciate the vitality of Catholic biblical interpretation and, like Protestants, Catholics strongly encourage the faithful to study Scripture with fervor and scholarly rigor.

Unfortunately, most fundamentalists do not distinguish the difference between the Catholic and Protestant polemics of the Reformation with modern ecumenical relations. In order to justify their rejection of the scriptural basis of Catholic tradition, they still incorrectly assert that Catholics don't read the Bible.

Q. Maybe Catholics are officially encouraged to read the Bible, but it doesn't seem that many know much about it. What does this say about the Catholic Church's unofficial treatment of the Bible?

Catholic education does not typically advocate the fundamentalist chapter-and-verse remembrance of Bible. Nevertheless, many Catholics today are students, readers, and pray-ers of the Bible; some have not yet become part of the "Catholic Bible movement," but they cannot avoid the overriding presence of the Bible in the liturgy and parish life. Any Catholic bookstore you enter these days is well stocked with bibles and books about the Bible, ranging from books for beginners to works of technical scholarship. Liguori Publications, the publisher of the book you are now reading, is only one among many Catholic publishers that distribute the Bible and publish numerous books about it. In addition, Catholic communities around the world sponsor Bible study for adults and children. Along with their Protestant and Jewish colleagues, Catholic biblical scholars are ranked among the best in the world. People who have the impression that Catholics are not "Bible Christians" might do well to take another look.

Q. What about the Catholic Church incorporating beliefs and practices that originated in the pagan world? That seems a very clear example of compromising the truths of Christianity.

This desire for purity in Christian belief and practice is admirable. However, this attitude overlooks the following two points:

1. There is no such thing as a pure, pagan-free Judeo-Christian tradition. From the first book of the Bible to the last, one can find adaptations of *pagan* ideas and imagery. The author of the Book of Genesis, for example, borrowed heavily from *Mesopotamian* mythology for his Creation account. And *Mesopotamian* demonology influenced the Jewish belief in demons that was so prevalent during Jesus' time. Recall that the faith of the *Ninevites*, who were non-Israelites, showed Jewish readers how to be faithful to God. *Greek* metaphysics encouraged Jewish hopes for an afterlife. Saint Paul's borrowed from *Stoic* lists of virtues and vices. The faith of the *Gentiles*—like Cornelius the *centurion* as recorded in Acts 10—helped the apostles themselves to understand that Jesus was not only for the Jews.

2. From the above, it is obvious that pagan influences have enriched Judeo-Christian religion and the Bible itself. Among Christian faiths, the Catholic Church stands out for its continuing openness to the wisdom of the non-Christian world, thus heeding the advice of Paul in Philippians 4:8: "Whatever is true, whatever is honorable, whatever is just, whatever is pure, whatever is pleasing, whatever is commendable, if there is any excellence and if there is anything worthy of praise, think about these things."

Plato and Aristotle, for example, have significantly influenced Catholic theology from its earliest days. During the past century Catholics recognized new facets of truth and divine revelation through ongoing dialogue with non-Christian philosophers, scientists, and even other world religions. Through all of this, the message of revelation remains unchanged, but the understanding of revelation continues to be immensely enriched.

Q. This openness to dialogue with pagans still sounds like a very dangerous practice. How can one prevent things from getting out of hand?

While Catholic theologians engage in a wide variety of dialogues that lead to groundbreaking discoveries of faith, the official teaching authority of the Church works constantly to discern truth and falsehood. Theological writings that are unfaithful to Scripture and sacred Tradition are continually critiqued by the ecclesiastic hierarchy of bishops—including the pope, his advisors, and the entire body of bishops—along with the assistance of lay and ordained professional theologians and historians. The *Imprimatur*—an official statement that a book does not violate official Church teaching on Christian faith or morals—appears on the copyright page of printed works intended for the faith instruction of Catholics, assuring readers that they are not being led astray. Fundamentalists, who do not accept the Church's teaching authority, do not have the assurance that comes from this source. Not having such assurance, some fundamentalists are naturally suspicious of any teachings and practices that seem to them not to adhere to the literal words of Scripture. In contrast, Catholics believe that the Holy Spirit is leading the Church into the fullness of truth (John 16:13), so the faithful are not preoccupied with censuring their leaders.

3

Teaching Authority
and the Papacy

Catechism of the Catholic Church:
77, 442, 552–553, 765, 816, 857–896, 1576

Q. Our discussion about Scripture and Tradition made it clear that Catholics look to a teaching authority for acceptable beliefs and practices. Who holds this teaching authority?

The teaching authority in the Catholic Church has been entrusted in a special way to the bishops. As the bishop of Rome, supreme pontiff of the universal Church, and apostolic successor to Peter, the pope is the pastor of all the faithful.

All of the bishops are successors of the apostles, who were the authoritative teachers in the early Church. Together with the pope, the bishops have the mission of continuing the pastoral work of Christ, the Teacher and Shepherd of the entire Church.

Q. You say that the authority of bishops derives from their apostolic roots. Is there any scriptural basis for recognizing the teaching authority of the apostles?

Passages that allude to their authority include: Luke 6:12–16; Matthew 28:18–20; John 20:21–23; 2 Thessalonians 2:15; 1 Corinthians 12:28–31.

Q. What is the basis for recognizing bishops as successors to the apostles?

Although the New Testament books were written very early in the life of the Church, distinctions had already been made between the ministries of deacons and elders (or elder-presbyters). The qualifications and duties for each are described in 1 Timothy 3. During the Apostolic Age, churches were governed by the apostles—hence, "Apostolic" Age. Later, community elders assumed this role, many of whom were appointed by an apostle or his delegate (see Titus 1:5). Eventually, the Greek word *episkopos* (overseer) signified the person appointed as a successor of the apostles. The English word *bishop* also shares this pastoral root.

By the beginning of the second century, clear distinctions existed between the roles of bishops, presbyters, and deacons. According to Ignatius of Antioch (AD 110), the duties of the laity were already understood:

> [The faithful] must all follow the bishops as Jesus Christ follows the Father, and the presbytery as you would the Apostles....Let no one do anything of concern to the Church without the bishop.
>
> *LETTER TO THE SMYRNAEANS, 8. 1*

Q. Why were bishops accorded such an important role? Why not a more democratic form of leadership?

By the second century the early Church had already learned the hard way that its unity depended on recognizing authoritative leadership. As Jewish-Christians and Gentile-Christians struggled to clarify the meaning and message of Jesus among a largely non-Christian population, heresies (false teachings) quickly surfaced. Only the stabilizing influence of the apostles and then the bishops prevented the Church from splintering beyond recognition. Unlike secular democracy, the first bishops had to preserve divine truth by boldly proclaiming the gospel amid unbelief and criticism. So when disputes and misunderstandings arose in the early Church, they did not take a vote; rather they appealed to the words and teachings of the apostles who had been so close to the Lord. Again, the idea is that the leaders of the Church—yesterday, today, and tomorrow—propagate the message of Scripture. Bishops shepherd the faithful, but their authority comes from God.

Q. But it is Jesus who is the Way, the Truth, and the Life—and the Bible is his Word. Why not simply look to the biblical Jesus for guidance and to the early Church for an organizational model?

Those who model discipleship solely upon the biblical Jesus and the witness of his first followers must recognize the wide array of leadership models presented by Scripture and the early sources. So-called bible-based communities, however well intentioned, tend to select one organizing principle from Scripture to the detriment of all the others, thereby causing fragmentation with other Christians who are not organized in the same way. Unfortunately (or fortunately, depending on one's perspective), Scripture does not present a neat, tidy picture of the mission and meaning of Jesus with respect to ecclesiastic structure. The organization of the early Church described in the New Testament is far from uniform. The Church at Philippi, for example, seems to have been somewhat hierarchical, while the Church in Corinth divided responsibilities among charismatic leaders. The early Jerusalem community held all their possessions in common (see Acts 2:44–45), but in other communities there seems to have been private ownership of property (see 1 Corinthians 16). One might think that the New Testament documents would provide an adequate basis for unity in the Church, but that is simply not the case. Scripture is not a static governmental manual; rather, it provides a dynamic way of living and loving, one that is best understood through the Holy Spirit as it has been passed through the leaders of the Church.

Q. What about the pope, then? Why do Catholics believe in the pope?

Catholics do not "believe in" the pope. Catholics believe in Jesus Christ as the Lord and Savior of humanity. Catholics look to the pope for teaching and leadership.

Q. What is the basis for recognizing the authority of the pope?

The Scriptures themselves point out the significance of Peter's leadership. He speaks for the apostles on several occasions (see Matthew 8:27–29; John 6:67–69; Acts 2:14–36). And Peter is commissioned by Jesus to be leader of the Church (see Matthew 16:18–19 and Luke 22:31–32).

Q. Surely the first Christians did not consider Peter to be a pope in the modern sense? In Galatians 2:11–14, Paul shares an account of how he corrected Peter on one occasion.

As was the case with the role of bishop, the papacy attained its developed status in post-biblical times. The title "pope" is derived from the Greek *pappas*. The title "Holy Father," which Catholics call the pope, is a close translation of the word. In the West, the term *pope* has been reserved for the bishop of Rome since the sixth century. Still, the leadership of the bishop of Rome has been considered normative since the second century. As the arbiter of disputes between churches, the bishop of Rome helped the Church maintain its unity. Peter, whose martyrdom at Rome served to establish the preeminence of that Church, came to be considered the first pope.

It is true that Paul opposed Peter during the famous dispute at Antioch over the issue of Jewish Christians eating with Gentile Christians (Galatians 2:11–14). However, Paul did not go to Antioch to discredit Peter; rather, out of respect for Peter's position in the Church, he wanted to understand why Peter preferred to minister to Jewish Christians and not Gentile Christians. As it turned out, Peter's preference came from his respect for the Gentiles and their culture. As Tertullian noted in AD 200, according to Paul, "[Peter's] fault certainly was one of procedure and not of doctrine" (*The Demurrer Against the Heretics*, 23, 10). In the end, they both preached the same doctrine to different people; one to Gentiles and another to Jews. Paul questioned Peter's method, not his authority.

Q. Why was the bishop of Rome accorded such status? Why not the bishop of Jerusalem?

Because Peter and Paul ministered and died in Rome, and because Rome was the political center of the Mediterranean world at that time, it is understandable that the bishop of Rome would be accorded a special role in the Church. There is little doubt, however, that the bishop (apostle) of Jerusalem also played a very important role in the early Church (see Acts 15).

Q. Did all of the early churches submit to the authority of the bishop of Rome?

No, they did not. At one point, in the year 191, for example, Pope Victor I came close to excommunicating (excluding from the Church) the Christians of Asia Minor for not agreeing to celebrate Easter on a Sunday rather than on the fourteenth day of the Jewish month Nisan. The tension between the Roman and Eastern churches was aggravated by the imperial promotion of Christianity as the official Roman state religion in AD 315 and by the consequent power and prestige accorded the papacy. Ultimately, however, the Eastern church separated itself from Roman leadership over theological issues. They formally separated in the eleventh century.

Q. It is one thing to recognize the leadership of the bishop of Rome, but quite another to believe that the man is infallible. How do Catholics explain this?

Christ gave to the Church the task of proclaiming his Good News (Matthew 28:19–20). Christ also promised us his Spirit, who guides us "into all the truth" (John 16:13). That mandate and promise guarantee that we, the Church, will never fall away from Christ's teaching. This inability of the Church as a whole to stray into error regarding basic matters of Christ's teaching is called *infallibility*. The term *infallibility* means "immunity from error," a guarantee that a particular Church teaching on faith and morals (*fides et mores*) is error-free. In other words, infallibility describes how the

Church teaches without error those truths that are necessary for salvation.

Because the pope's responsibility is to be a source of Church unity, he has a special role in regard to the Church's infallibility; he is its key instrument. And so, the infallibility with which the whole Church is gifted belongs to the pope in a special way. This gift from the Spirit is called papal infallibility, but it must always be understood with respect to the entire Church (The Church, 12, 25). Several passages in the New Testament that focus on related concepts show an early understanding of this gift (see Luke 10:16; 1 Timothy 3:15: Matthew 18:18; and especially Matthew 16:17–19). The idea of papal infallibility as a norm for the Church was initiated during the thirteenth and fourteenth centuries. It finally became a formal Catholic dogma at Vatican I (1870) and was reconfirmed with respect to the whole Church at Vatican II (1963–1965).

Q. So the pope decides what Catholics believe?

No, that way of speaking paints a false picture, because it leaves out the importance of the Holy Spirit and the Christian community. Infallibility is a gift of God to the Church. Along with the pope, the bishops as a group also possess this gift. As Vatican II states, "The infallibility promised to the church is also present in the body of bishops when, together with Peter's successor, they exercise the supreme teaching office" (The Church, 25). Furthermore, recalling that the pope and bishops are the voices of the authentic *sensus fidelium*, the "consensus of the faithful," and that the faithful are the Church, we can rightly say that it is the Church, under the guidance of the Spirit, which proclaims what is and what is not authentic Catholic belief. As Vatican II states: "The whole body of the faithful who have received an anointing which comes from the holy one (see, for example, 1 John 2:20 and 27) cannot be mistaken in belief" (The Church, 12). In other words, the pope does not define infallible doctrine without the body of the faithful (including lay and ordained ministers).

Q. Is the pope always infallible?

It is only when the pope officially speaks *ex cathedra* ("from the chair"), as supreme shepherd and teacher of the universal Church, and to the universal Church—proclaiming by a definitive act some doctrine of faith or morals—that he speaks infallibly. When a pope speaks in this way, his teaching's immunity from error does not necessary depend on formal consent from the Church; it is a gift to the Church from God. Nevertheless, by definition, an infallible pronouncement defines doctrine concerning faith and morals to be held by the whole Church. As the center of ecclesiastical unity, the pope teaches infallibly through the Spirit on behalf of all the faithful.

Q. What are some examples of these infallible teachings?

Since 1870, the only infallible doctrine that has been proclaimed *ex cathedra* is the Assumption of Mary. The pronouncement was made by Pope Pius XII on November 1, 1950, after consultation with the bishops of the world.

This does not mean, however, that the Catholic Church does not view other doctrines in the same light of assurance. The doctrine of the Trinity, for example, has never been proclaimed *ex cathedra*, but it surely holds such status and would be proclaimed as such if there were ever a need to do so.

Q. Do you mean that all those papal writings on birth control, social justice, and other matters are not infallible statements?

Papal writings, such as encyclicals (letters), bulls (official documents), and statements by conferences (regional committees) of Catholic bishops are authoritative documents. But they are not statements proclaimed *ex cathedra* by the pope. These documents are expressions of the Church's authentic teaching, however, and Catholics are obliged to study them and put them into practice.

Q. Is the pope expected to make any infallible statements in the future?

Under the guidance of the Holy Spirit, the pope may make infallible statements on matters of faith and morals that are critical for salvation. For example, if a moral issue began to split the Church, the pope and the other bishops of the world might conceivably find it necessary to speak in that way.

Q. During those times when there were two or three popes, which one was infallible?

This is a rhetorical question usually asked in a spirit of sarcasm. A rhetorical answer might state that only the pope who was the true bishop of Rome rightly enjoyed the assurance of infallibility.

Q. If a Catholic does not believe in the doctrine of papal infallibility, is that person in "bad standing"?

It is important for Catholics to recognize the special role of the pope. As the shepherd of shepherds, and successor of Peter and the apostles, the pope naturally commands the respect of the faithful. In fact, without acknowledging the special role of the pope and bishops as teachers of the Church, it is questionable why one would want to be a Catholic at all. To deny infallible pronouncements (*ex cathedra* or not) is to deny critical matters of faith and morals, which could place one in "bad standing."

Q. Must a Catholic believe in the Assumption, the only infallible statement *ex cathedra*?

This doctrine that Mary, the Mother of Jesus, was taken body and soul into heavenly glory after her death is rooted in traditions dating back to the early Church. The formal pronouncement by Pope Pius XII (1950) was not especially a decision of the pope on a disputed question. Instead, the Assumption was firmly rooted in the Church's pious sense of belief. The main theological basis of the Assumption is that Mary, the Mother of Jesus, "found favor with

God" (Luke 1:30) because she "believed" (Luke 1:45) and, therefore, she is the perfect model of discipleship (John 17:25; 12:26). The ultimate end of Mary was determined by her sharing with Christ in salvation. Regarding the assumption of her body, one recalls the words of Paul: "So it is with the resurrection of the dead. What is sown is perishable, what is raised is imperishable" (1 Corinthians 15:42f.). Her Immaculate Conception, divine motherhood, and perfect discipleship warrants belief in her bodily glorification. For Catholics, she is hope for union with Christ. In light of this theology, one might rightly ask, "Why shouldn't Catholics believe in the Assumption of Mary?"

Q. Who elects the pope?

In the early centuries of Christianity, the pope was chosen by the clergy and faithful of Rome. Influenced by historical events over the centuries, the manner of electing popes has evolved into the current practice: the pope is now elected by the cardinals of the Church in a meeting called a conclave, which usually takes place in the Sistine Chapel at the Vatican. The election is done by ballot, a process which sometimes goes on for several days. When a candidate receives a two-thirds plus-one vote majority and then accepts that choice by the cardinals, he officially becomes pope. The public celebration known as the papal inauguration takes place at a later time.

Q. What are cardinals?

The word *cardinal* comes from the Latin *cardo*, meaning "hinge." It is an apt designation, for cardinals are persons chosen by the pope to be his key assistants and advisers in administering Church matters. As a group, they form the Sacred College of Cardinals. Originally, the first so-called cardinals of the sixth century were priests in charge of major churches in Rome. According to current Church law, a person must be a priest or a bishop before receiving the cardinalate. In the United States the archbishops of some of the great archdioceses such as New York, Chicago, and Los Angeles are customarily appointed to the rank of cardinal.

Q. Why do Catholics call their priests "Father," when Jesus expressly prohibited such a title being conferred upon others (Matthew 23:9)?

In the passage in question, Jesus also prohibited his followers from using the titles "rabbi" and "teacher" or "master." It is doubtful that Jesus intended to relegate these common words to the domain of the specifically divine. Clearly, this passage in Matthew (23:1–12) calls more for a total centering on the teaching of Christ than it does for the mere avoidance of certain words.

Q. But the term *priest* is a significant deviation from presbyter. *Priest* suggests rituals and sacrifices, but Christ has offered himself as the definitive sacrifice.

The English word *priest* is derived from the Greek word *presbyter*, which was only used to describe the ministry of the elders in the apostolic and post-apostolic Church (before the eighth century). The priesthood with respect to the notion of sacrifice was denoted by a completely different term in Greek, *hiereos*, which does not have an English translation. The question, in other words, begins with a conveniently mistaken assumption.

4

Salvation

Catechism of the Catholic Church:
161, 163, 169, 1213–1274; 1440–1445

Q. Why does the Catholic Church reject the doctrine of justification by faith alone when the Bible teaches this quite clearly in many places?

Actually, the Catholic Church does teach that faith is required for salvation, only Catholics have a different understanding of what this means and how this works than do some Protestant traditions. As the *Catechism of the Catholic Church* notes in #161, "Believing in Jesus Christ and in the One who sent him for our salvation is necessary for obtaining that salvation." And in #163, "Faith makes us taste in advance the light of the beatific vision, the goal of our journey here below. Then we shall see God 'face to face,' 'as he is.' So faith is already the beginning of eternal life."

Q. Maybe that's the official teaching of the Catholic Church on faith, but it doesn't seem like the leaders encourage Catholics to have a personal relationship with Jesus, or to know him as their Lord and Savior.

Popular Catholic devotions, prayers, and the Mass encourage a close, personal relationship with Jesus. The morning offering prayer, for example, which most Catholics learn at some time, gives expression to a surrender of oneself and one's day to God. At every Mass, we have our own version of an "altar call" as Catholics come forward to receive Christ most intimately in holy Communion. If some Catholics don't develop a personal relationship with Christ in the manner emphasized by fundamentalists and other Protestant groups, it's not because the opportunities for doing so aren't presented to them throughout the years of their faith development. Since Catholics believe that the faithful constitute the body of Christ, their relationship with Jesus is always framed with respect to their love for their neighbor. In other words, to be in relationship with Jesus is to be in relationship with others.

Q. What about salvation and good works? Don't Catholics also believe that good works are necessary for salvation?

We do emphasize the importance of good works, but not as ways of "earning grace" or salvation. Our belief is that works are the good deeds of love that, after justification, grow out of faith and are the measure of how we will be judged.

Q. Where does the Bible mention the need for good works?

The importance of works of mercy is powerfully affirmed in Matthew 25:31–46. Matthew 7:21–23 also suggests that faith and spiritual power count for nothing if they produce only lip service. The Letter of James states quite bluntly: "Faith by itself, if it has no works, is dead" (2:17).

Q. But it is Jesus who saves, not our good works. Salvation by works is impossible to attain for we cannot work our way up to God!

Again we note that the Catholic Church does not teach that we are saved by doing good works; but, rather that the gift of justification in faith must be confirmed and become fruitful in our works. As James 2:18 puts it: "Show me your faith apart from your works, and I by my works will show you my faith."

Q. Not all people who do good deeds are Christians, though, so it doesn't follow that good works necessarily give testimony to faith. Some do-gooders are even atheists, or people who belong to non-Christian religions. There can be no doubt that such people will be damned.

It is clear that Christ's coming was intended by God to lead us to heaven, but it is not for us to judge the reasons why some "do-gooders" have not accepted Christ in faith. One reason that the majority of people in the world are not Christian is simply that they have never heard the Gospel in an environment conducive to faith. Undoubtedly, there are many, too, who have rejected Christ because they were exposed to a perverted example of Christianity or a gross misrepresentation of the Gospel. God alone judges who shall be saved and damned. As Christians, it is our responsibility to continue to present non-Christians with the Gospel in an inviting and understandable manner.

Q. Are you saying that it might even be possible for people from other religions to be saved?

The Bible itself affirms as much while calling people to faith in Christ. In the Old Testament many passages speak of God's love for non-Israelites. For example, in Genesis (12:2; 17:9) and in Isaiah (2:2–5; 49:6, 22; 60:3), among other places, the nations find salvation through Abraham and Israel. Amos 9:7 affirms that Yahweh cares for people of other nations, such as the Philistines and Arameans (Syrians), as much as he cares for the Israelites. In chapter 3 of Jonah, the pagan Ninevites are saved not because they change their religion (they do not change it) but because they cry out to *Elohim* and undergo moral conversion.

In the New Testament, Acts 10 speaks of Cornelius who was a holy man even before his baptism. In Acts 10:34–35, Peter himself remarks: "I truly understand that God shows no partiality, but in *every nation* anyone who fears him and does what is right is acceptable to him" (emphasis added). And the classic passage, 1 Timothy

2:3–4, says: "This is right and acceptable in the sight of God our Savior, who desires everyone to be saved and to come to the knowledge of the truth."

In light of the above, it is not startling to find Vatican II stating that sincere non-Christians are "moved by grace" to know God's will "through the dictates of their conscience," that there is "good or truth" in their lives, and that Christ "enlightens all men and women that they may at length have life" (The Church, 16). Vatican II goes on to say that even people who have never heard the Gospel have "faith" and should be "associated with this paschal mystery"—the death and resurrection of Jesus (Decree on the Church's Missionary Activity, 7; Church in the Modern World, 22).

Of non-Christian religions such as Hinduism and Buddhism, which developed quite independently of Judaism and Christianity, Vatican II speaks with great reverence, saying: "The Catholic Church rejects nothing of what is true and holy in these religions" which "often reflect a ray of that truth which enlightens all men and women" (Declaration on the Relation of the Church to Non-Christian Religions, 2). The same document goes on to speak with equal reverence of Islam—which contains elements of both Judaism and Christianity—and Judaism, the root from which Christianity itself sprang.

So, yes, the Catholic Church, faithful to the Bible and sacred Tradition, teaches that people of other religions can be saved. This is true to our understanding of God's salvific will for the whole human race.

Q. Doesn't this teaching create a conflict with the teaching of the Bible? In John 14:6, Jesus says: "I am the way, and the truth, and the life."

If there were such a conflict, would there not also be a conflict between John 14:6 and the assertion of Jesus' close friend Peter in Acts 10:34–35? The truth is that there is no such conflict, for all who are saved are saved by Christ. It may help our faith-understanding to recall that Christ touches all human lives through creation.

That is, all things were created through the Word who maintains them in existence—see John 1:1–4 and 1 Corinthians 1:24; Colossians 1:15–17. The Word became flesh and, as announced at Vatican II, through this action "he [Jesus], the Son of God, has in a certain way united himself with each individual" (Church in the Modern World, 22). Furthermore, Christ is risen; he is at this moment present to all human beings, offering grace and salvation. So, even for people who have never heard his name, Jesus is the Way, the Truth, and the Life. Their consent to him and the guidance of his Spirit in their conscience implies a kind of faith—call it *implicit faith*, as distinguished from *explicit faith* such as we find among believers in the Church.

Q. This seems like a very dangerous idea! If people can be saved by what you're calling implicit faith, then what is the need for the Church or missionary activity? Why not simply let them live out their lives wherever they are and be saved through this implicit faith?

The answer to this is something upon which all fundamentalists should agree; namely, that it is the greatest of blessings to know Christ as one's Lord and Savior, and so all people should be invited to this wonderful relationship. Second, implicit faith enables one to more consciously and willingly cooperate with God's plan for humanity and the earth by embracing the Gospel and its moral and spiritual imperatives. In Christ Jesus, we see more clearly what is sometimes only obscurely hinted at in other religions, and so it is much better to live in the full light of the revelation of God. There is plenty of incentive here to justify evangelization and missionary activity. We learn from Vatican I that the purpose of revelation is to allow the truth to be known by all, with ease, with certainty, and without error (*CCC* #38).

Q. You mentioned forgiveness of sins in the context of this discussion of salvation; once a person becomes a Christian, he or she is completely forgiven. Do you believe this?

Although conversion marks the beginning of a new life in grace, it does not bring about the complete cessation of sin in the life of an individual. Christians are indeed forgiven—the slate of the past wiped clean!—but because we also continue to sin we must continually seek and accept God's forgiveness. God's forgiveness empowers us, then, to forgive ourselves and other humans the wrongs done to us, enabling us, in turn, to accept the grace of God—through Jesus—that leads to salvation.

Q. Where in the Bible does it say anything about salvation and forgiveness?

In Matthew 18:21–22, Jesus tells Peter that he must continually forgive those who wrong him. In the parable of the unforgiving debtor (Matthew 18:23–35), Jesus goes on to point out that God will deal with us mercifully if we deal likewise with one another. He also states that God will judge harshly those who do not extend forgiveness to others.

Q. All right, so God wants us to forgive one another and seek forgiveness of sins from God; this is part of living a life of faith. But why do Catholics believe that confession to a priest is so important?

According to Father Eamon Tobin's, *The Sacrament of Penance*:

In response to this question, the first remark I often make is, "Why do we not object to having a mediator, another man, at the Sacrament of Baptism. Why don't we just baptize ourselves?" Baptism, among other things cleanses us of sin. The Sacrament of Reconciliation is like a second Baptism; it cleanses us of post-baptismal sin. If we have no objections to another man's mediating God's grace to us in the Sacrament of Baptism, why should we object to another man's mediating God's grace in the Sacrament of Reconciliation?

The primary reason, however, why the Catholic Church asks her members to confess their sins to a priest is simply because the Church has always believed that sin, however private, is a community affair. Every sin, however small, wounds the Body of Christ, the members of the Church. When we are baptized we are grafted onto the Body of Christ. If my hand is infected, before long my whole body feels the effect of that infection. No part of the human body can suffer pain without all parts being diminished or affected. What is true of the human body is also true of the Body of Christ (the Church). When any of its members sin, they all suffer. Moreover, through my sins I diminish the light of Christ in the larger community. Because my sins wound the community and diminish its effectiveness, reconciliation must include the community and not just God. In the confessional the priest is the representative of God and the community. In the confessional the priest represents the whole Christ, the Head (Jesus) and the members (the Church).

Q. This seems heretical. God alone can forgive sins. How can you claim that a priest can forgive?

We know that Jesus himself forgave sins (see Luke 5:17–26), that he gave his Church authority to do likewise (see John 20:22–23), and that the early Church exercised this authority in various ways (see Matthew 18:15–20: Luke 7:47; 1 Corinthians 5:1–5; 2 Thessalonians 3:14–15; James 5:15–16; 1 Peter 4:8). In all these Scripture passages, what we see is that God forgives sins through the ministry of Christ, and that such forgiveness is perpetuated throughout the ages in the Church. In other words, Jesus *is* the agent of forgiveness for the Church.

During the second through fifth centuries, reconciliation developed into a public process, due largely to the Church's need to deal with serious sins, such as murder, apostasy, and adultery. The penitent received absolution and reincorporation into the community only after the bishop and the community were satisfied with the depth of the penitent's new conversion. During the sixth to twelfth centuries, the practice of one-to-one confession by laypeople to monks was prominent. This practice provided the benefit of private spiritual counseling. During the twelfth to fifteenth centuries, the Church spelled out doctrinal and moral matters with great precision; it was during this period that theologians, such as Thomas Aquinas, stated that confession of sins to a layperson—a practice in the Church from the earliest times—was not a formal sacrament in the same way as confession to a priest. During the sixteenth century, however, the reformers broke with the Roman Church and thus gradually changed the perception that priestly confession was a sacrament instituted by Christ. Even after that, however, Martin Luther, one of the most influential reformers wrote:

> We teach that confession is an excellent thing....If you are a Christian you will go on your own....If, on the other hand, you despise it, and if you are too proud to confess your sins, we conclude that you are no Christian....So when I urge the practice of confession, I am but urging every man to be a Christian.

As in so many matters, fundamentalism (and some other Protestant traditions) broke with the Christian practice of confession established during the early Church.

Q. In the sacrament of penance, or reconciliation, why does the priest give a penance? How does one earn God's forgiveness by doing penance?

The practice of giving a penance—often in the form of prayers or offerings—after confessing is not to earn God's forgiveness, for this is a grace freely given by God out of mercy. The purpose of the penance is, ideally, to help strengthen the penitent against further instances of temptation. In this sense, penance provides spiritual discipline in order to develop holiness.

Q. What do Catholics believe about baptism and salvation?

Baptism is the rite of initiation into the Church, which is the Body of Christ in space and time. As the *Catechism of the Catholic Church* explains:

> The Lord himself affirms that Baptism is necessary for salvation. He also commands his disciples to proclaim the Gospel to all nations and to baptize them. Baptism is necessary for salvation for those to whom the Gospel has been proclaimed and who have the possibility of asking for this sacrament (#1257).

Q. So what does this tell us about non-Christians and salvation? Earlier you said there might be a chance that they could be saved, but now it seems that you're saying baptism is necessary for salvation.

The statement above from the *Catechism* notes the necessity of baptism for those to whom the Gospel has been proclaimed and who have the possibility of asking for this sacrament. In other words, if one hasn't even heard the Gospel, then it is understood that the lack of opportunity for baptism cannot be held against him or her. It is also possible that some have heard the Gospel, but adverse cultural traditions such as the threat of torture prevented them from assenting to baptism. In such cases, the implicit faith of such people is accompanied by what the Church has called the "baptism of desire," assuming that, given a fair chance to hear and respond to the Gospel, they would choose baptism. There is also a "Baptism of blood" recognized for "those who suffer death for the sake of the faith without having received Baptism" (*CCC* #1258).

Q. Why do Catholics baptize infants when it is obvious that they are incapable of making an act of faith?

The practice of infant Baptism is an immemorial tradition of the Church. There is explicit testimony to this practice from the second century on, and it is quite possible that, from the beginning of the apostolic preaching, when whole 'households' received baptism, infants may also have been baptized (*CCC* #1252).

Of course, there is also, here, a recognition of the role of baptism in healing the wounds of original sin.

The sheer gratuitousness of the grace of salvation is particularly manifest in infant Baptism. The Church and the parents would deny a child the priceless grace of becoming a child of God were they not to confer Baptism shortly after birth (*CCC* #1250).

Father Richard McBrien offers the following perspective on the baptism of infants:

Just as one enters a family by birth and is really a part of that family even though for a long period of time there is no real capacity for giving human love but only for receiving it, so one may be brought into the family of the Church before he or she is capable of understanding its significance or of expressing the love that marks this community out as the Body of Christ and the Temple of the Holy Spirit. In the case of infants, the intention is expressed not by the child but by those who bring the child for baptism—for example, parents, sponsors, relatives, and friends (*Catholicism*, 742–743).

Q. Why do Catholics often sprinkle with water at baptism instead of immersing the initiate as they did in the early Church?

The Catholic Rite of Baptism speaks of baptism "by immersion of the whole body or of the head only" and of baptism "by infusion or pouring." Pouring became by far the most common way, probably because of the practice of infant baptism; it would be dangerous to hold a baby underwater. Most modern Catholic churches are not built to accommodate baptism by immersion, but it is allowed provided that "decency and decorum" prevail. Increasingly, newer churches have a baptismal fountain where total immersion is possible, even for adults and older children. Immersion is not viewed as more efficacious, however, than infusion or pouring.

Q. Why do Catholics baptize "in the name of the Father and of the Son and of the Holy Spirit" instead of "in the name of the Lord Jesus" as Acts 19:5 prescribes?

In Matthew 28:19, Jesus commissions his apostles to baptize using the familiar Trinitarian formula. Because Jesus is the Son, the Catholic formula of baptism implicitly includes "the name of the Lord Jesus." The baptismal wording used in Matthew reflects the practice of the second-generation Church in Antioch, where Matthew's Gospel was written. We note, here, too, that many fundamentalist churches also use the Trinitarian formula.

Q. What has Holy Communion got to do with salvation?

Jesus says, "Very truly, I tell you, unless you eat the flesh of the Son of Man and drink his blood, you have no life in you" (John 6:53). Catholics believe that this passage refers to the bread and wine offered at the Lord's supper (Mark 14:22–25), which Jesus enjoined us to partake of in memory of him (Luke 22:19). This memorial is celebrated in every Catholic Mass.

Q. But the Lord's Supper is only a memorial meal. He did not intend for us to take his words so literally, did he?

It is surprising that fundamentalists do not adopt a literal interpretation of Scripture for this important topic. But let us save our discussion of the Catholic Mass for the next chapter. We are discussing salvation here, and we have the words of our Lord from John 6:53 to meditate upon now.

Q. Is salvation assured to those who do all that you have described?

God's will is for the salvation of all people. But even Paul, the great apostle, warns us: "Work out your own salvation with fear and trembling" (Philippians 2:12). In the latter part of his life (around AD 56), Paul did not consider that he had yet won "the prize" (see Philippians 3:10–15). We should be sobered by the thought that conversion does not guarantee us unending fellowship with Christ (see that frightening discourse in Hebrews 6:4–8). But we may also be consoled in knowing that nothing can separate us from the love of God (Romans 8:35–37) and that those who persevere in faith and love until the end will be saved (Matthew 10:22; 24:13).

Salvation is a gift from God: it is our truest human destiny. But it will require from us the death of selfishness in our lives (Luke 9:23–24). Thus will the cross of Christ become part of our journey to heaven.

Q. We cannot conclude this discussion without asking about purgatory. Where did this non-biblical notion come from?

Catholics believe that if you die in the love of God but still possess some "stains of sin," such impurity is cleansed away during the process of purgatory. Purgatory is not a place but a stage or process in the afterlife. In this stage the dead are aided by the prayers of the living, a biblical datum contained in 2 Maccabees 12:39–45 and passed on by the early Christians as part of our tradition from Judaism. The doctrine was well-established in the Church by the second century.

Having passed through purgatory, one becomes utterly unselfish, capable of perfect love. The selfish ego—that part of a person that restlessly seeks self-satisfaction—will die forever. Here individuals are transformed and purified by the intensity of God's love.

Implied in this doctrine is a universal bond between the communion of saints and the people of God, including those on earth and those who have gone before us. Vatican II focused on this bond by saying that it "accepts loyally the venerable faith of our ancestors in the living communion which exists between us and our sisters and brothers who are in the glory of heaven or who are yet being purified after their death" (The Church, 51).

Q. Finally, what about limbo?

The idea of limbo is that infants who die unbaptized go to a state in which they are eternally excluded from the beatific vision of God, but are not conscious of the exclusion and so enjoy a "natural beatitude." Belief about limbo has no explicit biblical basis and has never been part of official Church teaching. Nevertheless, the idea developed through the Middle Ages and into the twentieth century. Today it seems untenable to many theologians and faithful because of a deepened conviction that God's love and grace are with us from the first moment of our existence. Therefore, "the Church can only entrust them [infants] to the mercy of God, as she does in her funeral rites for them" (CCC #1261).

5

The Mass and
Holy Communion

Catechism of the Catholic Church:
1322–1405; 1544–1553, 2177–2179, 2180–2183

Q. Why are Catholics supposed to go to Mass every Sunday?

Keeping holy the Lord's day is a practice that goes back to Jewish observance of the Sabbath. Christians changed this day from Saturday to Sunday because that is the day the Lord rose. Catholics attend Mass every Sunday out of fidelity to this tradition of communal worship.

Q. But why does your communal worship take the form of the Mass? Why not simply pray, sing, and preach?

Catholic Sunday liturgy includes congregational singing, preaching, and times for silence and communal prayer. The Liturgy of the Word, the first part of the Mass, is very much like most Protestant services. There are times for song, readings of Scripture passages from the Old and New Testaments, and then preaching by a priest or deacon to help the community live out the scriptural message. Unlike most Protestant services, however, Catholic worship then goes on with the Liturgy of the Eucharist. This memorial of the Lord's Supper is done in fidelity to the words in Luke 22:19.

Q. So the Liturgy of the Eucharist in the Mass is simply a memorial service? That is what we believe, you know.

Catholics do believe that the Eucharist is a memorial, but in a sacramental sense—that is, signifying the actual saving presence of

Jesus. As the following quotation from Vatican II shows, the term *memorial* in the Catholic understanding means a great deal more than simply a remembrance. The second chapter of the *Constitution on the Sacred Liturgy,* "The Most Sacred Mystery of the Eucharist," begins with these beautiful words:

> At the last supper, on the night he was betrayed, our Savior instituted the eucharistic sacrifice of his body and blood. This he did in order to perpetuate the sacrifice of the cross throughout the ages until he should come again, and so to entrust to his beloved spouse, the church, a memorial of his death and resurrection: a sacrament of love, a sign of unity, a bond of charity, "a paschal banquet in which Christ is received, the mind is filled with grace, and a pledge of future glory is given to us" (#47).

This mystery is the very center and culmination of Christian life. It is the source and apex of the whole work of preaching the Gospel. In every Mass, Christ comes in a very special way under the form of bread and wine; his death becomes a present reality, offered as our sacrifice to God in a sacramental way. Following the instructions of Jesus, as often as the sacrifice of the cross is celebrated, the work of our redemption is carried on.

Q. But aren't these words about eating Jesus' Body and Blood merely symbolic? I've heard that the words of consecration do not call for a literal interpretation of eating and drinking Christ's Body and Blood.

For Catholics, symbol and reality are not mutually exclusive. Catholics assert that Christ is really present in the consecrated bread and wine and that the faithful draw their understanding of this mystery from the teachings of Scripture and the ongoing guidance of the Spirit in our Tradition.

Q. What is the scriptural basis for believing that Christ is really present in the consecrated bread and wine?

In the Greek text of the New Testament, Mark 14:22, Matthew 26:26, and Luke 22:19 read as follows: *Touto estin to soma mou*. In the earliest account of the words of consecration 1 Corinthians 11:24—Paul's collocation is slightly different: *Touto mou estin to soma*. In each case, the English rendition is usually: "This is my body." Philologists tell us that the verb *estin* can mean either "is really" or "is figuratively." But Paul's discussion of the Lord's Supper in 1 Corinthians 11:23–34, which preceded Mark's Gospel by about eight years, reflects the belief that the presence is real, not merely figurative. Furthermore, the Greek word for body used in John 6:52–58 is *sarx*, which can only mean physical flesh and which scholars say is closer in meaning to the Aramaic word *bisra* that Jesus himself used. Further evidence that the early Church believed in the presence of Jesus in the sacrament comes from Bishop Ignatius of Antioch, writing in AD 110. Speaking of certain people who hold "heterodox opinions" contrary to "the mind of God," Ignatius says: "They abstain from the Eucharist and from prayer, because they do not confess that the Eucharist is the Flesh of our Savior Jesus Christ, Flesh which suffered for our sins and which the Father, in His goodness, raised up again (*Letter to the Smyrnaeans*, 6, 2). A figurative and exclusively symbolic interpretation of the words of consecration does not reflect the practice of the early Church nor Catholic belief. Nevertheless, the Catholic Church does not deny the symbolic function of the Eucharist—a dynamic understanding of symbol makes the mystery of the real presence possible. As Augustine explains, there is an intimate connection between a sign and the thing signified—for example, between the bread and wine of the liturgy and its manifestation of the real body and blood of Jesus.

Q. But how can bread and wine become Christ's Body and Blood? It does, after all, still taste like bread and wine.

C. S. Lewis put it well when he wrote, "The command, after all, was 'Take, eat': not 'Take, understand.'" Christ's presence in the form of bread and wine, and how it comes to be that way, is part of the mystery of faith we call the holy Eucharist. The official Catholic teaching is that Christ is really present in the consecrated elements. The explanation known as "transubstantiation" says that the substance of bread and wine is changed into Christ's Body and Blood, leaving only the appearance, taste, and so on, of bread and wine. But at the heart of this belief is an opening to mystery that Saint John Chrysostom expressed very well when he wrote: "It is not man that causes the things offered to become the Body and Blood of Christ, but he who was crucified for us, Christ himself. The priest, in the role of Christ, pronounces these words, but their power and grace are God's" (*CCC* #1375).

We might note, here, that Christ's presence during Mass isn't limited to the consecrated bread and wine, although that is the mode in which he is present "in the fullest sense: that is to say, it is a *substantial* presence by which Christ, God and man, makes himself wholly and entirely present" (*CCC* #1374). In addition, he is present in the gathered community, in the reading of the Scriptures, in the person of the priest, and even in the altar. When we are open to receiving him in all these modes of presence, we have a much fuller and richer experience of him in the Mass.

Q. Why do Catholics call the Mass a sacrifice?

"Acting in the person of Christ and proclaiming his mystery, they [priests] unite the votive prayers of the faithful to the sacrifice of Christ their head, and in the sacrifice of the Mass they make present again and apply, until the coming of Lord (cf. 1 Corinthians 11:26), the unique sacrifice of the New Testament, Christ offering himself once for all an unblemished victim to the Father (cf. Hebrews 9:11–28)" (The Church, 28).

Q. Why bring in the idea of sacrifice to a simple memorial meal?

To refer to the Lord's Supper as merely "a simple memorial meal" is to lack memory of its roots. To understand the Eucharist, we must remember that Jesus is a Jew. The Jewish Temple had a sacrificial liturgy which the synagogue did not have. Besides the Passover sacrifice of the Paschal lamb, other Temple sacrifices took place frequently. One of these sacrifices was the *Zehah Todah* (*Zehah* = sacrifice; *Todah* = communion) in which a meal was shared with God. Part of the *Zehah Todah* sacrifice was burnt up at the altar, and part of it was given back to the offerer who then ate it with friends. The sacrifice was also a meal. The eucharistic prayer of the Mass is kind of like that; it is not just a blessing before a meal, but a true sacrifice. The meal is a sacrifice in the tradition of the Jewish *Todah*.

The Lord's Supper was, in addition, a Passover meal, a Jewish sacrificial rite recalling that the angel of death "passed over" those homes marked with the blood of an innocent lamb (see Exodus 12). Christians came to recognize Jesus as the Lamb anticipated in the Passover rite (Hebrews 9:15) whose suffering led to our salvation. It was at this Passover meal that the apostles ate and drank the bread and wine given to them as his Body and Blood, "my blood of the covenant, which is poured out for many" (Mark 14:24). The Lord's Supper, now celebrated in memory of Jesus at every Mass, turns our attention back to Calvary and forward to his ultimate coming. As Paul wrote in 1 Corinthians 11:26: "As often as you eat this bread and drink the cup, you proclaim the Lord's death until he comes."

Q. But the Bible states quite clearly that the one sacrifice offered by Jesus suffices completely for the atonement of sin (Hebrews 10:11–12). Catholics seem to go against this Scripture by sacrificing Christ anew every day.

Catholic doctrine affirms that the one death of Jesus broke the hold of sin. It is precisely from this one sacrificial death that the

Lord's Supper and, hence, the Mass, draws its significance. There is no conflict with the Scripture you cite.

A concept that might be helpful here is *anamnesis*, which means literally, "not forgetting." The remembrance of Christ's passion and death during the Mass is such an anamnesis, only in a very distinctive way. Here we not only remember the deeds of Christ done long ago, but through this anamnesis, we actually touch them in our present time. When the priest consecrates the bread and wine, he speaks in the person of Christ the very words spoken by Christ at his last supper with the disciples: "This is my Body....This is my Blood...do this in memory of me." Christ himself is speaking these words, offering the same gift to us that he offered to his disciples so long ago. And it is the same sacrifice of Calvary that we touch through anamnesis: Christ's saving presence encountering us across the bridges of time. "In this divine sacrifice which is celebrated in the Mass, the same Christ who offered himself once in a bloody manner on the altar of the cross is contained and offered in an unbloody manner" (*CCC* #1367).

Q. I have heard the Mass has changed many times through the ages, so isn't this new emphasis given by the Catholic Church to elevate the status of the clergy?

The core beliefs that Jesus is truly present under the form of bread and wine, and that the Mass is a sacrificial remembrance of Calvary as described above are not new, but have been with the Church from the beginning. Some aspects of the Mass have indeed changed through the ages, however. Providing a comprehensive history of the Mass is beyond the scope of this work, so I will leave it to the reader to investigate this in more depth.

Q. What role does the priest play during Mass?

The priest is the celebrant; he leads the community in worship. Describing the roles of the priest and the people in the Eucharist, Vatican II says: "In the person of Christ he [the priest] brings about the Eucharistic sacrifice and offers it to God in the name of all the people. The faithful indeed, by virtue of their royal priesthood, share in the offering of the Eucharist" (The Church, 10).

Q. Is it the priest or the community who consecrates the bread and wine?

It is God, through the action of his priest, who does it. The official prayers of the Church make this quite clear. The priest prays to God the Father:

> Bless and approve our offering;
> make it acceptable to you,
> an offering in spirit and in truth.
> Let it become for us
> the body and blood of Jesus Christ,
> your only Son, our Lord.
>
> *EUCHARISTIC PRAYER I*

> And so, Father, we bring you these gifts.
> We ask you to make them holy by the power of your Spirit,
> that they may become the body and blood
> of your Son, our Lord Jesus Christ,
> at whose command we celebrate this Eucharist.
>
> *EUCHARISTIC PRAYER III*

Q. Why are only priests and bishops allowed to preside at the Eucharist? Why not other holy people?

This privilege is theirs by virtue of their role or office in the Church. From this standpoint personal holiness does not enter into the question, although it is certainly desirable that holy men preside at Mass. This should not be an especially controversial issue, for religious communities of every faith recognize special roles for their ministers.

Q. Are priests and bishops, then, mediators of sorts between God and humanity?

They represent both Christ and the community when they preside at Mass, so they are mediators in the sense that they occupy a middle position.

Q. But 1 Timothy 2:5 states that there is only one mediator between God and humanity, and that is Jesus Christ.

That is correct, but there is no contradiction between Catholic teaching and this Scripture passage. The priest is not presenting himself as an alternative to Christ, but as one who represents Christ, especially when ministering the sacraments. It is Christ who is the true cause of the efficacy of the sacraments, not the priest. "In the ecclesial service of the ordained minister, it is Christ himself who is present to his Church as Head of his Body, Shepherd of his flock, high priest of the redemptive sacrifice, Teacher of Truth. This is what the Church means by saying that the priest, by virtue of the sacrament of Holy Orders, acts *in persona Christi Capitis*" (*CCC* #1548).

We also note, however: "This presence of Christ in the minister is not to be understood as if the latter were preserved from all human weaknesses, the spirit of domination, error, even sin" (*CCC* #1550). So the Church is not saying that priests and bishops are to be regarded as perfect likenesses of Christ in their personal lives—only that when they are in the role of administering the sacraments, it is Christ who is ministering to the Church.

Q. The subject of mediators brings up the special role you claim for Mary as mother and mediator.

See next chapter, please.

6

Devotion to Mary
and the Saints

Catechism of the Catholic Church: 828, 946–959, 963–973,
1717, 2030, 2156, 2634–2636, 2683–2684

Q. Why do Catholics believe that prayers to Mary are better than any other kind?

Catholic doctrine makes no such assertion about the efficacy of prayers to Mary. Many Catholic prayers invoke the intercession of Mary, and Vatican II encouraged "urgent supplications to the Mother of God and of humanity" (The Church, 69). But such intercessory prayers are ultimately directed to Jesus; for, while honoring Christ's Mother, these devotions ensure that her Son "is rightly known, loved and glorified and his commandments are observed" (The Church, 66).

Q. Doesn't this special regard for Mary really interfere with reverencing Christ? Isn't it in fact true that many Catholics pray more to Mary than to God?

As Vatican II recognized, there have been excesses in devotion, and even narrow-mindedness regarding Mary at different times and in different places. That is why the Council Fathers encouraged theologians and preachers to "rightly illustrate the offices and privileges of the Blessed Virgin which always refer to Christ, the source of all truth, sanctity, and devotion" (The Church, 67). Nevertheless, as the *Catechism of the Catholic Church* notes, the special devotion given to Mary "differs essentially from the adoration which is given to the incarnate Word and equally to the Father and the Holy Spirit, and greatly fosters this devotion" (#971). Perhaps it is true that some

Catholics pray more to Mary than directly to God, but it doesn't follow that this leads them away from God or that their prayers aren't ultimately directed to God.

Q. What about that passage from 1 Timothy 2:5, then, which states that Jesus alone is our Mediator? Why treat Mary as a mediator, too?

We touched on this point briefly in our last chapter, acknowledging that Christ alone is the absolute mediator between God and humanity. Still, the Bible is filled with encouragements for the faithful to pray for one another (Matthew 5:44; Romans 15:30; Ephesians 6:18–20: 1 Timothy 2:1–4). Indeed, "since Abraham, intercession—asking on behalf of another—has been characteristic of a heart attuned to God's mercy. In the age of the Church, Christian intercession participates in Christ's, as an expression of the communion of saints" (*CCC* #2635). The Bible, in other words, urges us to be mediators through intercessory prayer. Mary, and all those who have died in Christ, now enjoy a special relationship with the Lord. Asking Mary or a saint to pray for us is similar to asking a friend to keep you in his or her prayers. In the case of Mary, we have a very special person indeed—the woman whose obedience led to the birth of Christ himself. "Mary's role in the Church is inseparable from her union with Christ and flows directly from it. 'This union of the mother with the Son in the work of salvation is made manifest from the time of Christ's virginal conception up to his death…'" (*CCC* #964). Prayer to Mary is ultimately directed to Christ, her Son, who in turn mediates for us with the Father.

Q. Why not go directly to Christ in prayer?

The Catholic Church emphatically encourages people to turn directly to Christ in prayer. That some people choose also to ask for prayers from their friends in heaven—Mary and the saints, who together constitute the communion of saints—is a good thing, provided it doesn't lose its ultimate focus in Christ.

Q. But the Bible does not venerate Mary the way Catholics do. In fact, Jesus seems cold and abrupt toward her at times (Mark 3:31–35; Luke 2:46–50; John 2:1–4), and the prophet Jeremiah actually cursed her (Jeremiah 7:18).

First of all, Jeremiah, in deploring devotion to the "queen of heaven," was not alluding to Mary at all but to Ishtar, the Assyrian goddess of fertility.

Second, the Gospel passages in question do not indicate disrespect on Jesus' part, but his own consciousness of a mission that superseded mere social conventions. He seized those moments not so much to reprimand Mary but to make her and others more aware of his true mission.

Finally, it must be pointed out that Scripture does great reverence to Mary. She is called "blessed...among women" and "the mother of my Lord" (Luke 1:42–43), and "all generations" will call her "blessed" (Luke 1:48). Jesus was obedient to her and Joseph (Luke 2:51), and lovingly cared for her needs even from the cross (John 19:26–27). She is the only woman mentioned by name among those who waited for the Holy Spirit (Acts 1:14). These references indicate a special place for Mary in the heart of the early Church.

Q. Why do Catholics exaggerate this special regard for Mary in the Bible by maintaining further that she was always a virgin? Matthew 1:24–25 suggests that she and Joseph had marital relations after the birth of Jesus, and Jesus' brothers and sisters are alluded to in Matthew 13:55–56 and other places.

On this point, *The Jerome Biblical Commentary* acknowledges "the implication, easily taken in English, is not present in the Greek participle (*heos*), and still less if we suppose a Semitic background of the passage. The New Testament knows nothing of any children of Mary and Joseph." Matthew 1:24–25 is primarily interested in stating that Joseph is not the father of Jesus. The phrase "until she had borne a son" does not necessarily assert the commencement of marital relations after Jesus' birth: it is merely stressing the reality of the virginal conception.

In Matthew 13:55 and other passages alluding to the brothers and sisters of Jesus, it is not clear that the relatives in question are also the children of Mary; Jesus is the only child of Mary mentioned in Scripture. The Jewish meaning of the Greek word in question is *brethren*, which includes relatives as well as brothers and sisters. If Jesus had brothers and sisters, then one must ask why he commended Mary to the care of John (John 19:27). Finally, sacred Tradition attests to the perpetual virginity of Mary in writings that go back as far as AD 358 (see Athanasius, *Discourses Against the Arians*, 2, 70). This is one of many examples where Tradition is needed to help us come to a more complete understanding of the meaning of Scripture.

Q. What about the Immaculate Conception? There's nothing about that in Scripture, and if Mary was supposedly free from sin, then why did she refer to God as her Savior (Luke 1:47)?

The germinal roots of the dogma are hinted at in the Annunciation passage, where the angel Gabriel calls her "blessed among women" (Luke 1:28), and in the Scriptures attesting to the sinfulness of all people (Romans 5:12–14) and the sinlessness of Jesus (Hebrews 4:15). Eventually, it became necessary to explain how Jesus, "a man like us in all things but sin," could have been born of a woman and still remain free from original sin. Thus it was that the Church came to proclaim that Mary, from the moment of her conception, was free from original sin and possessed justifying grace in a manner similar only to our first parents (Adam and Eve) and her Son. This is why she is called the new Eve.

Lest we feel that Mary enjoyed graces that we are denied, it should be noted that baptism breaks the hold of original sin no less than did Mary's Immaculate Conception. Yet who among the baptized will deny our need for a Savior? Mary realized that God was the source of all saving grace.

Q. Is the Assumption of Mary somehow linked to these recent doctrines?

These "recent doctrines" were part of the Church's understanding of salvation history for centuries before the Protestant Reformation. Although solemnly affirmed during the past 130 years, the dogmas of the Immaculate Conception and the Assumption of Mary are not new Catholic "inventions."

The Assumption of Mary derives from an early reverencing for her empty tomb. The implications of this belief were clearly expressed as early as the seventh century. Basically, this belief states that "when the course of her earthly life was finished, [Mary] was taken up body and soul into heavenly glory, and exalted by the Lord as Queen over all things, so that she might be the more fully conformed to her Son, the Lord of lords and conqueror of sin and death" (*CCC* #966). Mary's Assumption assures us of our own eventual bodily resurrection. But we, who are conceived in the state of original sin, must await the final fruits of baptism, the final resurrection of the dead.

Q. If Mary leads to Jesus, and Jesus mediates God's grace, why do Catholics also venerate the saints?

Vatican II reviews the classic reasons for veneration of the saints in the following statement:

When we look on the lives of those women and men who have faithfully followed Christ we are inspired anew to seek the city which is to come (see Hebrews 13:14 and 11:10), while at the same time we are taught about the safest path by which, through a changing world and in keeping with each one's state of life and condition, we will be able to arrive at perfect union with Christ, which is holiness. In the lives of those companions of ours in the human condition who are more perfectly transformed into the image of Christ (see 2 Corinthians 3:18). God shows, vividly, to humanity his presence and his face. He speaks to us in them and offers us a sign of this kingdom, to which we are powerfully attracted, so great a cloud of witnesses are we given (see Hebrews 12:1) and such an affirmation of the truth of the Gospel.

It is not only by reason of their example that we cherish the memory of those in heaven; we seek, rather, that by the practice of fraternal and sororal charity the union of the whole church in the Spirit may be strengthened (see Ephesians 4:1–6). Exactly as christian communion among pilgrims brings us closer to Christ, so our communion with the saints joins us to Christ, from whom as from its fountain and head flow all grace and life of the people of God itself. It is most fitting, therefore, that we love those friends and co-heirs of Jesus Christ who are also our sisters and brothers and outstanding benefactors, and that we give due thanks to God for them, "humbly invoking them, and having recourse to their prayers, their aid and help in obtaining from God through his Son, Jesus Christ, Our Lord, our only Redeemer and Savior, the benefits we need."

THE DOGMATIC CONSTITUTION ON THE CHURCH, 50

Q. But Psalm 6:5 states that "in death there is no remembrance." If this is so, then why believe that the saints can hear our prayers and intercede for us?

This psalm was written hundreds of years before Jewish and Christian thought about resurrection of the dead and afterlife came to the fore. The psalm does not refer to heaven, about which nothing was known at the time, but to Sheol, that realm of the afterlife to which Christ descended and preached the good news. The psalmist, like many of the Old Testament writers, could not foresee the developed tradition that would be evident later in the New Testament.

Q. Isn't the whole matter of recognizing saints a bit farfetched anyway? The Bible uses the word *saints* to refer to believers. Why do Catholics use the word only in reference to holy men and women?

The veneration of holy Christian men and women goes back as early as the third century. It is likely that the usage of the word *saint* evolved through time to refer, eventually, only to those men and women who were exemplary models of what it means to be a believer. It is, however, acceptable to use the word in the biblical sense, that is, in reference to all believers. "By *canonizing* some of the faithful…the Church recognizes the power of the Spirit of holiness within her and sustains the hope of believers by proposing the saints to them as models and intercessors" (*CCC* #828).

Q. How does a person officially become recognized as a saint by the Catholic Church?

Through a process known as *canonization*, the pope—in consultation with the body of the faithful—officially recognizes individuals who died as exemplary models of faithfulness and virtue. Many saints are recognized for their death in defense of the Church or others for their unselfish, uncompromising dedication to the gospel throughout their life. Final canonization occurs after a previous process called *beatification*, which includes an investigation of the person's life, writings, and posthumous miracles. If a person is martyred, no miracles are required. Saint Martin of Tours, who died in AD 397, was one of the first non-martyred saints—a so-called "white martyr," because there was no bloodshed at his death. The Church considers all persons who are in heaven to be saints, not only those officially canonized and not only Catholics and other Christians.

Q. Devotions to certain saints do not seem to meet the criteria you just mentioned. Remember Saint Christopher, patron of travelers? He didn't even exist! And what about Saint George, slayer of dragons?

In early centuries, popular acclaim was sometimes sufficient to give rise to a person's veneration as a saint. There are, indeed, numerous instances of legends and devotions lacking credible historical substance. Catholic scholars have discovered the truth about a number of such cases and are working to discover the truth about others. The painstaking and rigorous process used for canonization today was not always the practice. The steps and norms of the present-day process can be found in the enactment regarding canonization promulgated by Pope Paul VI in 1969.

Q. What about patron saints? Where did this idea come from? It's not in the Bible.

Many saints became identified with the special causes for which they worked during their lives. This is partly why Christians who work for the same causes seek those saints' intercession; they know that the saint in question has "been there, done that," as a popular saying goes, and will empathize with their continuing struggle to realize the ideals for which he or she worked. A good example of a patron saint for good works is Saint Vincent de Paul, who labored on behalf of the sick, the aged, convicts, and babies deserted by parents.

Q. But why bother with this practice of intercessions through Mary and the saints? As Hebrews 4:15–16 puts it, we now have in Jesus Christ one who knows and understands our human situation completely and who pleads for us constantly at the right hand of the Father. Who needs more than this?

What you say here is true, and more Catholics than ever are turning directly to Jesus in prayer instead of going through Mary and the saints. This recent shift probably derives from a growing appreciation for the humanity of Jesus, which many theologians tended to de-emphasize in centuries past. It is the human Jesus who makes God accessible to us; neglect of Jesus' humanity leaves people with a sense that he is remote and unapproachable, thus giving rise to a compensatory veneration of saints. Although a healthier Christology is taking root, it would be a shame if we were to lose our appreciation for our friends and relatives in the communion of saints.

7

Creation, Evolution,
and Original Sin

Catechism of the Catholic Church: 282–314; 396–412
Also see, Truth Cannot Contradict Truth (TCCT): address
by Pope John Paul II to the Pontifical Academy of Sciences,
October 22, 1996.

Q. Why is the theory of evolution taught in Catholic schools?

The theory of evolution is considered by scientists to be a cred-ible explanation for the diversification of life forms. As Pope John Paul II noted in his address to the Pontifical Academy of Sciences:

[During the past fifty years a] new knowledge has led to the recognition of the theory of evolution as more than a hypothesis....It is indeed remarkable that this theory has been progressively accepted by researchers, following a series of discoveries in various fields of knowledge. The convergence, neither sought nor fabricated, of the results of work that was conducted independently is in itself a significant argument in favor of this theory

TRUTH CANNOT CONTRADICT TRUTH, #4

Catholic teachers of science would be terribly remiss if they withheld exposure to it from their students.

Q. Doesn't evolution conflict with belief in God as Creator?

Not necessarily. The Catholic Church condemns all philosophies, including those based on the theory of evolution, which deny the ultimate dependence of creatures on God (*CCC* #285). But the theory of evolution does not necessarily lead to atheistic conclusions, as Darwin himself pointed out many times. Catholic theologians today affirm belief in God as Creator while pointing out that evolution is the process through which God created the human body.

Again it is Pope John Paul II who brings clarity to this issue:

> If the human body take its origin from preexistent living matter, the spiritual soul is immediately created by God. …Consequently, theories of evolution which, in accordance with the philosophies inspiring them, consider the spirit as emerging from the forces of living matter or as a mere epiphenomenon of this matter, are incompatible with the truth about man. Nor are they able to ground the dignity of the person.
>
> *TRUTH CANNOT CONTRADICT TRUTH, #5*

Q. But the Book of Genesis states that God created the world in six days! Evolutionists maintain that it took billions of years for life to evolve to its present state. What shall we believe—God's word or the word of fallible human scientists?

Highly respected Scripture scholars—Jewish, Protestant, and Catholic—are convinced that the authors of Genesis did not intend to write, and did not write, a scientific treatise on the Creation of the universe. What they wrote is a book that sets forth religious truths. The process of creation described in Genesis is suited to a world-view that is no longer adequate. Furthermore, Scripture scholars tell us that the six-day account of Creation is a mythological way of acknowledging that the multitude of inanimate and animate forms owe their existence to God's creative Word and that humanity is the crowning glory of Creation. When one realizes that the six-day account was never intended to present a scientific and historical point of view, the apparent conflict with evolutionary theory vanishes.

Catholic teaching, as well as the teaching of most other major

Christian and Jewish groups, holds that the evolutionary theory need not be incompatible with the Genesis account of Creation. Scientific observation of evidence that God has given us (see Romans 1:20), which led to the theory of evolution, offers an explanation of the ways of God's universe.

Q. How can any Christian believe that anything in the Bible is a myth?

One must not equate myth with falsehood or with imaginary nonsense. An entirely different definition of myth (see a dictionary) applies to traditional stories, parables, and allegories. As such, myths communicate truth, but in a symbolic or metaphorical vein; they are not intended to be interpreted literally. For example, Jesus' parable of the sower and seeds (Matthew 13:4–9) is interpreted symbolically by everyone—even fundamentalists! Scripture scholars from many Christian denominations have long recognized the mythical qualities of Genesis, although its revelation of the place of God as Creator is in no way diminished by this.

Q. This sounds like a dangerous practice! Why not simply interpret the Bible literally?

Because it was not written to be understood literally. The Bible does convey religious truth without err, but we must reflectively discern what is the essential truth communicated and what is accidental. The Bible contains a variety of forms of literature: poetry, songs, proverbs, prayers, prophecies, parables, epistles, gospels, genealogies, and historical narratives, to name a few. Biblical interpretation must take into account the type of literature being studied as well as the historical and cultural circumstances during which the work was written. Only then will we be able to get at the authors intentions and understand the meaning of their work in the light of Scripture as a whole (Dogmatic Constitution on Divine Revelation, 12).

Q. So you say Genesis is a literary myth and does not necessarily conflict with evolution. Are you saying that human beings evolved from lower apes?

Evidence from fossils, DNA, anatomy, and physiology strongly suggests our relatedness to other primates, including earlier forms that have become extinct. But this does not detract from the fact that we are conscious of being creatures who can actually dialogue with the Supreme Being whom we "image" (Genesis 1:27), that we are creatures who can say to God, "What are human beings that you are mindful of them, / mortals that you care for them" (Psalm 8:4)? What "theistic evolution" affirms is that God made use of the evolutionary process to form the human body and specially to create a spiritual soul for each individual who is conceived.

Q. If human beings evolved, then what do we do with the story about Adam and Eve?

The story of the Fall (Adam and Eve) from grace is part of divine revelation. "The account of the fall in *Genesis* 3 uses figurative language, but affirms a primeval event, a deed that took place *at the beginning of the history of man*. Revelation gives us the certainty of faith that the whole of human history is marked by the original fault freely committed by our first parents" (*CCC* #390). In that sense, "Adam and Eve" represent our first truly human parents.

Q. So are you saying that Adam and Eve really existed, or are they only symbolic parts of what you're calling a myth?

In the light of revelation, we affirm the existence of first humans who were given a spiritual soul that was directly created by God. Whether God bestowed this blessing on only one, two, or more people, we do know for sure, but there is reason to believe that God could have done this through a first man and woman, who are called Adam and Eve in the Bible. In fact, there are some studies of genetics that point to a single female ancestor for the whole human race.

On the other hand, it is clear that Adam and Eve represent

symbolic names that need not be applied to individuals. Adam means "man" or "from the earth." Eve means "helpmate." Hence, their story could also be construed to mean the fall of man and woman—the human race.

Q. How can you regard Adam and Eve as only symbolic people and still accept the doctrine of original sin?

First, Catholics do not claim that they are "only symbolic people." The Genesis account might or might not be referring to two individuals, but that wouldn't affect the outcome. The Church's teachings on original sin (which fundamentalists by and large accept) were defined before we understood much about our origins; it was inevitable that the early Fathers assert a monogenic (two-parent-only) context for their teaching. Some modern versions of the evolutionary theory suggest a polygenic (multiple-parent) origin and a gradual development of human characteristics. As scientists continued to amass a wide variety of data strongly confirming the evolutionary hypothesis, theologians began working more freely on the polygenic alternative. Although no polygenic explanations have been given full affirmation, theologians have pointed out that God may well have chosen only one male and female out of a humanoid population to bear the consciousness of his image and likeness. In that view, the Adam and Eve story is reaffirmed; their sin spreads to affect others with whom they and their offspring eventually interbreed. Pope Pius XII in *Humani generis* affirms that original sin "proceeds from a sin actually committed by an individual Adam and which, through generations, is passed on to all and is in everyone as his own" (#37).

Q. These seem like such farfetched ideas! Why not simply scrap the theory of evolution and use as our model the theory of scientific creationism, which at least squares well with Genesis?

Space does not permit a comprehensive response to this question. Suffice it to say the following:

1. The Genesis account of Creation should not be taken literally, owing to its mythical-literary nature. It is therefore unnecessary to look for scientific confirmations of its six-day account.
2. The theory of evolution is supported by data from a number of scientific disciplines, although many questions remain unanswered.
3. Scientific creationism is based upon weak and even erroneous information, and it neglects numerous facts which contradict it. That is why the overwhelming majority of scientist do not consider scientific creationism a credible hypothesis.

There is nothing in creation that suggests that the world was created by only God, as scientific creationists contend. Nature religions are generally polytheistic, which points out the indebtedness of scientific creationism on an a priori conclusion based on Genesis. This is, at best, very sloppy science!

Q. Evolution is still just a theory, which means that it might be wrong.

Well, not exactly. Evolutionary dynamics have been verified in many situations, including laboratory populations of bacteria and a wide range of plant and animal species. Scientists use the term *theory* in reference to it because it cannot be affirmed with the same degree of confidence as a scientific law. So to say that evolution is a theory and not a law doesn't imply that it's only some kind of a wild guess about how life has diversified through the ages. The quote by Pope John Paul II in response to the first question in this chapter summarizes the view among scientists very well.

Creation science, on the other hand, does not enjoy the wide range of acceptance that evolution does, and has been rebutted many times by evolutionists. It should also give us pause to note that most creation scientists are inclined to a literal interpretation of the book of Genesis. Creation science is called a theory by some of its promoters, but using that word doesn't imply that it has equal credibility to the theory of evolution among scientists and even theologians.

Q. But how could God be involved in evolution? Doesn't this belief detract from God's power?

Catholics believe that God created nature to function within certain laws—laws which science can explain. Deism, which flourished in the seventeenth and eighteenth centuries, maintained that creation unfolds apart from its disinterested Creator. It viewed God as being like a divine clock-maker who wound up the universe and then left it to run by itself. Catholic theism, in contrast, asserts that God is active within creation. Nevertheless, God does not usually transgress the laws he set up; rather, he shapes creation through the power of his love, especially through loving people. This perspective does no dishonor to God's power, and also stresses his infinite patience in bringing creation along.

Those who believe that God acts directly upon and through nature must, by logical extension, blame God for hurricanes, droughts, volcanoes, earthquakes, and floods. Catholics do not believe that God causes natural disasters; they believe that these phenomena are part of the ordinary functioning of nature within laws we are equipped to comprehend, anticipate, and adapt to. Thus Catholics encourage scientists to learn everything possible about our world, that we might use our God-given minds to help make life better for all.

8

Second Coming and Last Judgment

Catechism of the Catholic Church: 440, 671–681, 830, 849, 988, 1038–1041, 1051–1052, 1060, 1107, 1130

Q. Do Catholics believe that Christ will come again, or is this just a symbolic way of speaking of the evolution of the human race?

Catholics believe Christ will be revealed in his glory at some time in the future.

> Though already present in his Church, Christ's reign is nevertheless yet to be fulfilled "with power and great glory" by the king's return to earth....That is why Christians pray, above all in the Eucharist, to hasten Christ's return by saying to him: *Marana tha!* "Our Lord, come!"
>
> *CATECHISM OF THE CATHOLIC CHURCH, #671*

Q. Is the Catholic Church more on the premillennial than postmillennial side when it comes to understanding the Second Coming?

Catholic teaching has elements of both pre- and postmillennial theology. For those who don't know what these terms mean in this context, they refer to the thousand-year reign of peace described in the Book of Revelation 20:1–7. Premillennialists believe that the Second Coming will take place prior to this thousand-year period and will, in fact, be the reason why this reign of peace is established. Postmillennialists, on the other hand, hold that the return of Christ will come at the close of a long period of peace and justice.

With the premillennialists, the Catholic Church teaches that the Second Coming of Christ will be a historical event that will usher in a new age. We would differ from some fundamentalists teachers in our belief that there is no millennial period between the Second Coming and the Last Judgment. According to Catholics, the two go together: when Christ comes, he will judge the living and the dead.

With postmillennialists, the Catholic Church emphasizes the importance of working to help the reign of God be known "on earth as in heaven." That does not mean that we endorse the classical postmillennial view that the Second Coming cannot take place until we have come to a reign of peace among ourselves.

In some ways, the Church is also a-millennialist (against millennialism) in that our teachings on the Second Coming are not premised in reference to the thousand-year reign of peace.

Q. What does the Catholic Church teach about the time and place of the Second Coming?

Following the teaching of our Lord (Matthew 24:42, Vatican II addresses the question of when the Second Coming will take place and expresses the Church's vision:

> We do not know the moment of the consummation of the earth and of humanity nor the way the universe will be transformed. The form of this world, distorted by sin, is passing away and we are taught that God is preparing a new dwelling and a new earth in which righteousness dwells, whose happiness will fill and surpass all the desires of peace arising in the human hearts....
>
> [During the time that is left to us], here that body of a new human family grows, foreshadowing in some way the age which is to come....
>
> When we have spread on earth the fruits of our nature and our enterprise—human dignity, sisterly and brotherly

communion, and freedom—according to the command of the Lord and in his Spirit, we will find them once again, cleansed this time from the stain of sin, illuminated and transfigured....Here on earth the kingdom is mysteriously present; when the Lord comes it will enter into its perfection.

PASTORAL CONSTITUTION ON THE
CHURCH IN THE MODERN WORLD, 39

The reign of God is already present in mystery. The day has already begun when God "will wipe every tear from their eyes. / Death will be no more." The day has already begun when he says to all living beings: "See, I am making all things new....It is done! I am the Alpha and the Omega, the beginning and the end" (Revelation 21:4–6).

Q. Our biblical prophets have interpreted the discourses about the Second Coming to indicate an event about to take place. Popular books such as *Late, Great Planet Earth* and the *Left Behind* series also describe the probable sequence of events based on the teachings of the Bible. Does the Catholic Church agree with these kinds of writings?

Not entirely. Catholics do agree with fundamentalists on what we might call the big picture—that we live in a time of history between the resurrection and Second Coming, that the Church will undergo a period of trials, and that the faith of many will be tested. But the highly detailed forecasts in the kinds of publications mentioned above do not seem an inevitable outcome of reflection on the Scriptures about the end times. Indeed, it often seems to us that fundamentalist scholars misunderstand the nature of those kinds of writings and read more into them about our future than was intended by the biblical authors.

Q. Are you suggesting, then, that many fundamentalist biblical scholars have misinterpreted the Scriptures about the end times?

In some cases, yes: especially those where detailed accounts are projected with Scriptures used as proof texts. What one must understand, here, is that the Lord's words about his Second Coming are couched in a special type of writing called *apocalyptic literature*. The Old Testament Book of Daniel—a message of hope for Jews enduring persecution under the Syrian King Antiochus—is a prime example of this type of writing. Apocalyptic literature such as the Book of Daniel, the New Testament Book of Revelation, and the accounts about the Second Coming in the synoptic Gospels (see Mark 13, Matthew 24, and Luke 21) employs striking symbolism to impart its message. Catholic theologians maintain that these writings are primarily a challenge to communities of that time to continue trusting in our sovereign God, even during times of persecution. The visions of God's eventual conquest described in these works seem to be more a summons to hopeful perseverance through a time of suffering that the community is actually experiencing than a tract making predictions about the future. In that context of tribulation, the projections about the future were written to affirm God's sovereignty and to assert with assurance that God's good outcome in history shall prevail.

Q. Are you saying that the symbols in books like Revelation do not apply to this age?

It is the genius of the Book of Revelation that its dragons, prostitutes, plagues, and other symbols apply to every age. Undoubtedly, the early Church took it to be a story of their own struggles with the Roman Empire; later ages found it to be relevant to their situations. There are certainly crises and circumstances in our own age into which one might plug the symbols of the Book of Revelation.

Catholic theologians do not object to the use of apocalyptic literature to fire our hopes for the Second Coming. What is objectionable is the use of apocalyptic literature to scare people into "belief" by postulating a world on the verge of collapse, out of which Christians shall be "raptured" away. Catholics also object to the fatalism about helping to change the world that follows in the wake of these beliefs. People who are too deeply engrossed with the end of time can be blind to present injustices staring them in the face. Such persons will not likely respond to the real needs of the neighbor in the here and now. But that is what the Last Judgment will really be about, on how we have treated our fellow human beings.

Q. Do Catholics believe in the rapture? Matthew 24:41 and 1 Thessalonians 4:16–17 clearly state that Christians will be raptured, or taken up to heaven in Christ, before the time of the great tribulation!

The "rapture" refers to the belief that Christians who are alive at the time of Christ's coming being taken up to meet him. Catholics have no dispute with this belief, and the Scriptures in question do seem to be references to the fate of the living at the time of the *Parousia*, or Second Coming. Fundamentalists take things a step further, however, by viewing the rapture as a kind of first stage of the Second Coming, with Christ withdrawing only those who are united with him from the earth, while leaving the rest behind to undergo a seven-year period of tribulation. After that time, they believe Christ will come again in a most glorious manner, ushering in the thousand-year reign of peace we referred to earlier as "millennium" theology. The popular *Left Behind* series of novels—fiction—takes this approach, for example, but most Catholic biblical scholars are doubtful that Matthew 24:41 and 1 Thessalonians 4:16–17 support this view of a two-staged Second Coming. Catholic ministers are also concerned about the way this teaching seems to be used by some fundamentalists to frighten people into conversion.

Q. What do you mean by suggesting that the teaching on the rapture is used to "frighten people into conversion"? We're just presenting what we understand the Word of God to be saying and we believe people really should know about the tribulations of the end times.

I'll respond to this one by describing an experience I had with rapture-based preaching in the late 1970s, when I was a campus minister at Louisiana State University. A popular evangelist named Josh McDowell delivered a series of teachings on Christianity and the end times to a packed house at the LSU Assembly Center. His presentation consisted of powerful lectures and slide shows graphically depicting the horrors (nuclear war, famine, pestilence, and so forth) of the seven-year period of tribulation that he was predicting to come in the very near future. Bible verses were quoted and related to current events as if supporting the truth of his predictions, and everything was presented as though the future he was describing was an irrefutable fact. After alerting us to the horrors to come, he moved into his evangelical appeal, emphasizing that those who are Christians will be raptured from this world before the tribulations and will not have to live through those times on the earth. His definition of what it meant to be a Christian emphasized a definite, unmistakable, born-again experience, and he invited students to come to the altar to testify to their faith.

For weeks afterwards, we counseled frightened Catholic students who were dismayed by the horrors of McDowell's end times and were doubtful of their own Christian faith. Many had been faithful believers and regular churchgoers for years, but could not recognize in their lives the kind of twice-born religious experience that had been described by McDowell. We replied with a series of lectures on a Catholic understanding of the end times and the Book of Revelation, and included here our understanding of salvation. All in all, it turned out to be a teachable time for the students at LSU, but I was still left feeling put off by how rapture theology is used to frighten people to coming to faith.

Q. How is that different from preachers teaching about hell and damnation? Catholic preachers have been known to use this tactic through the ages.

The difference is that the Catholic Church teaches very clearly that hell is a distinct possibility for those who take their spiritual lives too much for granted, or whose lives are ruled by sin. The theology of the rapture promoted by fundamentalists hardly enjoys the same standing as the teaching on hell. Nevertheless, you are right that scaring people to come to faith isn't unique to fundamentalists. Fortunately, most Catholic preachers have abandoned the fire-and-brimstone approach.

Fundamentalists also teach that the time of rapture and tribulation is very near at hand. Relating current events to the obscure symbolism in the Book of Revelation and other apocalyptic works can be done in any age. There is nothing particularly unique about this one in that regard.

Q. What about the blossoming of the fig tree in Matthew 24:32–33? Don't the crises of the day—nuclear weapons, terrorism, pollution, overpopulation, and so forth—seem like a blossoming of evil which only an intervention by God can rectify? Then there is the rebirth of the nation of Israel. The events of the last days described in the Bible refer to Israel as a nation, and that couldn't have taken place until recent history.

The crises of this age are indeed unique in that our failure to work through them could result in the annihilation of life on our planet, or at least very serious destruction of the environment. Even so, Christians should never doubt that the Holy Spirit can strengthen us and teach us to transform sinful situations into goodness. We desperately need God's intervention to save us, but it may be that he will work through our human nature rather than outside it. This is the true meaning of the Incarnation: grace transforming nature. Therefore, belief in the Second Coming should not lead to a passive waiting for the Lord's return (see 2 Thessalonians 3:6–12). Rather, we are to work and pray constantly to realize God's kingdom on earth as in heaven (Matthew 6:10) until Christ returns whatever this means and whenever and however it may become manifest.

9

Guidelines for Getting Along

It's really difficult to get along with a person who tells you that your religion is not good enough and that you'll probably go to hell if you don't quit your church. If this person is a family member, friend or coworker, this kind of criticism can seriously strain your relationship—even destroy it! Yet that's the reality facing many who rub shoulders with zealous fundamentalists on a regular basis.

Because nonfundamentalists do not talk about their religion the way fundamentalists do (a lingo some have called "Christianese"), and because Catholics and others from mainline Protestant denominations disagree with them on the interpretation of certain Scripture passages, fundamentalists often have real doubts about the orthodoxy and salvation of other Christians. Judgmental attitudes can be found among Catholics and Protestants, of course, but fundamentalists tend to be very intolerant of others whose beliefs differ from theirs, and they don't always express this in respectful ways.

Fortunately, not all fundamentalists are so narrow-minded. In his book, *Fundamentalism: What Every Catholic Needs to Know*, Anthony Gilles describes three kinds of attitudes among fundamentalists concerning their views of Catholicism:

The lunatic fringe. These are groups and individuals who hold ridiculous anti-Catholic positions such as those expressed in *Chick* comic books. Their belief is that the Catholic Church is not a Christian organization and that practicing Catholics are going to hell. The lunatic fringe also tends to be paranoid, favoring conspiracy theories in which the Catholic Church is associated with the Mafia, world governments, or the United Nations in its attempt to enslave the world.

The sophisticated bigot. This position attempts to assume a posture of loving concern for the well-being of the millions of poor, misguided Catholics who are being led astray by their Church. Actually, when you challenge this type using even respectful disagreement, a virulent anti-Catholicism raises its ugly head and refuses to dialogue about the most basic differences. In my opinion, the televangelist Jimmy Swaggart is a prime example of this type. Other fundamentalist TV preachers are not as blatantly anti-Catholic as Swaggart, but few, if any, of them say that Swaggart should tone things down a bit.

The informed moderate. Fundamentalists in this group are generally more open and respectful of Catholics, although they maintain many doctrinal differences. Gilles identifies the Reverend Pat Robertson as an example of this group. There are certainly many fundamentalist ministers and laypeople who are loving and respectful of others who hold views unlike their own.

Obviously, it is easier to get along with an informed moderate than a lunatic fringe type or a sophisticated bigot. There will be differences of opinion between Catholics and fundamentalist moderates, but these do not take away from our primary focus of loving one another as brothers and sisters in Christ.

On the other hand, it is very difficult to grow in a relationship with the other two attitudinal types. But what can be done about it? How can one get along with fundamentalists when, day after day, we have to interact with them. What follows are a few suggestions.

1. Examine Your Own Beliefs

Sometimes it takes a zealous fundamentalist to help us realize that we are pretty lukewarm about our Catholic faith. When this happens, it is only natural to get defensive and to discount the fundamentalist's words as those of a "Jesus freak." But what about the issue of your faith ? Do you know what you really believe about God? Christ? salvation? the Church? Can you explain your faith to a variety of groups—coworkers, atheists, children, or fundamentalists? No, this is not Father's job or Sister's responsibility. You stand for Christ wherever you are. The people you encounter might never make it to Father or Sister. Maybe you will be the one to reach them.

Rather than getting defensive when a fundamentalist alerts you to your unfamiliarity or halfheartedness, it would be a far more mature response to tell them that they're right—that you really don't know how to respond and that you really do need to grow in your faith understanding. To admit this does not mean that you have to switch churches, however. Do a little more searching in the Church in which you were raised. It is a serious thing to switch churches. One might as well try to change one's ethnic origins.

2. Respect Religious Rights

A person's right to worship God as he or she sees fit is one of the most basic human rights. Whether or not you agree with fundamentalists, it is essential that you respect their right to worship God in the manner they choose. The same holds true with regard to you, of course.

One of the most common questions that arises is whether it is better for the nonfundamentalist spouse to compromise and go to church with the fundamentalist spouse or to go to separate churches. This is a tough question to answer, but it is more important to be true to oneself before God than pretend to believe for the sake of some romantic notion of family togetherness in church. In other words, even within a marriage the integrity of one's faith response to God is of more importance than being with one's spouse in a pew on Sundays.

Questions concerning children and worship are another matter. Traditionally, the Catholic Church has insisted that children of interfaith marriages be raised Catholic. It is likely that fundamentalists (especially ex-Catholic converts) will be unsympathetic to this position. After all, what if their fundamentalist church wants children of interfaith marriages to be raised as fundamentalists? Perhaps a possible compromise here is to expose the children to both faiths, although this might be confusing for them.

3. Take Time to Listen

A fundamentalist maxim for others: "If you only knew...you would do as we have done in making Jesus our personal Savior!" Listening is the beginning of wisdom. Even though you may not agree with fundamentalists, it is important to hear what they have to say. Ask them about their experiences. What has happened to them? How did it change their lives! What precisely is it that leads them to believe they have encountered Christ or the Holy Spirit?

Many times, such "interviewing" questions will redirect their focus from "saving" you or preaching at you to actually communicating in a more respectful manner. By asking such questions you begin to practice "attentive listening." This kind of listening helps you to hear the other's feelings, and not just their beliefs and opinions. If you can respond in a way that connects with those feelings by showing that you understand why the other considers their experiences so important, you have made a vital personal connection.

Once people start talking about their experiences, there exists a real possibility for meaningful dialogue. Through listening, you might discover that you, too, have had similar experiences, and you may choose to share about these. This kind of interpersonal sharing is generally less contentious and disruptive to relationships than arguing about whose dogmatic beliefs are correct.

4. Remember That You Are Both Christians

I guess it is no secret by now that I have many problems with Jimmy Swaggart's theology. Nevertheless, I must acknowledge that he is a Christian a follower of Jesus Christ. He might not consider me to be a Christian (at least not a very good one), but that does not change the fact that I know I am a Christian, and I know that he is one, too.

What this means is that fundamentalists are our brothers and sisters in Christ. The *Dogmatic Constitution on the Church* of Vatican

II recognized that "in some real way they (Protestants) are joined to us (Catholics) in the Holy Spirit for, by his gifts and graces, his sanctifying power is also active in them" (#15). Christians are one in the Lord, and, if the truth be told, Catholics and other Christians probably agree about more things than they disagree. It is good to acknowledge points of agreement and to affirm one another as fellow followers of Christ.

5. Agree to Disagree

If you try all of the above and tensions persist, then it is time to agree to disagree. You might say something like, "Well, you believe this, and I understand where you're coming from. But I don't see it that way. There's probably no changing either of our minds in this area at this time, so let's just leave it be. I think it's in both our best interest to drop the matter and pray for understanding."

This is a very mature thing to do. By agreeing to disagree, we demonstrate that maintaining a loving relationship is more important than our need to be right. Christianity is about loving God and neighbor. Whenever a relationship is terminated because two Christians cannot agree about theology, I would guess the devil makes merry in hell.

6. Exercise Truthful Assertiveness

But what if the other continues to bring up controversial issues? What if they are unwilling to agree to disagree in the first place? Many fundamentalists cannot stand to leave unsettled questions open. Part of the reason for this is their concern for our salvation, but another is their own insecurity. The fact that you can be a Christian and not see things their way is very threatening to many fundamentalists because it causes them to question their own faith.

I have a relative who cannot talk about anything without turning it to religion. We can be watching a football game, and he will say something like, "Well, you know life, too, is like a struggle between two teams. There is God's team and the devil's...." As he rambles on, I can see the people around me grimacing. Sometimes people only want to watch a football game and leave it at that; we are not necessarily interested in making analogies between football and eternal life. What I have had to do in such cases is to say, "Please, Fred, I don't feel like talking about religion right now; I just want to watch the game."

There is nothing wrong with telling people what we like and dislike, especially if we do so in a simple, assertive manner. The alternative to this is the grimacing, or a blowup of some kind, or other detrimental expressions of feelings. As it happens, "Fred" is usually quite responsive to assertive statements.

7. Limit the Relationship

This is the most drastic of steps, but it sometimes cannot be helped. If, for example, Fred did not respond to my assertive requests, I probably would choose not to place myself in situations where he would disturb me. Another common situation arises when parents decide to keep their children from neighbors or relatives because the children have become the targets of heavy proselytizing. It is unfortunate that such things happen, but the reality is that some fundamentalists—especially those of the lunatic fringe type—simply will not relent in their efforts to "save" everyone. When this happens, the only way to avoid conflict is to avoid spending time with such persons.

8. Forgive the Person

No matter what anyone does, it is likely that fundamentalists will say things that hurt us, and vice versa. Remember that religious beliefs lie very close to one's self-concept; this is why religious discussion sometimes becomes very emotional. Criticizing a person's religious beliefs cuts to the heart. College children have wounded parents by saying they weren't raised as true Christians, and that they (the parents) are going to hell if they don't change churches. These things hurt!

If we do not practice forgiveness, withstanding such verbal abuse can lead to crippling resentment.

Forgiveness does not mean that we forget what the other did or that we ignore basic areas of disagreement. Forgiveness does not even mean that we have to continue to be in a relationship with a person who has hurt us. What forgiveness means is that we hold nothing against the other or that we let go of all resentments toward them. However justified these resentments may be, the fact is that the one who harbors resentment suffers just as badly as the recipient of this anger, probably more so.

9. Continue Being Considerate

Unless you decide to completely break off your relationship with a fundamentalist, it is a very good thing to simply continue relating on a basic human level. This means visiting when he or she is sick, remembering birthdays, sharing your everyday experiences, taking time to have fun together (if possible)—all those everyday kinds of contacts which are, after all is said and done, the real occasions for bonding in relationships.

Summary

It's not the end of the world if a loved one is a fundamentalist. Some people might be better off as fundamentalists; others become more inconsiderate and judgmental because of their strict brand of faith.

Fundamentalism challenges us to read the Scriptures and learn more about our faith. Perhaps God has sent fundamentalists into our lives to nudge us toward growth in faith. And perhaps God has placed you in the life of a fundamentalist to help him or her see that Christian faith and God's loving presence can be found in other Christian traditions.

In the end, however, Christian faith is not merely a matter of who has the right doctrine, but of empowering people to know God in Christ and to love as he loved. By persisting in the effort to love, it is likely that many fundamentalists will respond in kind. Some who have left the Catholic Church might even choose to return. If they do not return, however, we can ask God to fulfill their belief in Jesus the Savior.

References

A New Catechism: Catholic Faith for Adults. Crossroad, 1977. A straightforward presentation of post-Vatican II Catholic beliefs and practices. Commissioned by the Catholic Hierarchy of the Netherlands, with a special Supplement prepared under the direction of a Commission of Cardinals.

Brown, Raymond E., Joseph A. Fitzmeyer, and Roland E. Murphy, eds., *The New Jerome Biblical Commentary*. Prentice Hall, 1990. Includes verse-by-verse commentaries on each book of the Bible plus technical information on the evolution of each book and of the Bible as a whole. Also includes notes and comments by Catholic, Protestant, and Orthodox authorities.

Brown, Raymond E., *The Critical Meaning of the Bible*. Paulist Press, 1981. A modern reading of the Bible that challenges all Christian churches to be faithful to the Word of God.

Dulles, Avery, *Models of Revelation*. Doubleday, 1983. Explores revelation in Scripture and Church teaching, analyzing it as (1) doctrine, (2) history, (3) inner experience, (4) dialectical presence, and (5) new awareness.

Flannery, Austin, ed., *Vatican Council II: Volume 1, The Conciliar and Post Conciliar Documents, New Revised Edition*. Northport, NY: Costello Publishing Company, 1996.

_____. *Vatican Council II: Volume 2, More Post Conciliar Documents, New Revised Edition*. Northport, NY: Costello Publishing Company, 1998.

Gilles, Anthony. *Fundamentalism: What Every Catholic Needs to Know*. St. Anthony Messenger Press, 1986. A handy booklet describing the history of fundamentalism and basic fundamentalist criticisms of Catholicism.

Jurgens, William A., ed., *The Faith of the Early Fathers*. Liturgical Press, 1970. Three volumes, paperback. Letters and statements of belief written by Church Fathers from the first to the eighth centuries. Each volume contains scriptural, doctrinal, and general indexes.

Keating, Karl, *Catholicism and Fundamentalism: The Attack on "Romanism" by Bible Christians*. Ignatius Press, 1988. A classic work by one who spent lots of time "in the trenches" trying to dialogue with fundamentalists. Keating provides a detailed description of what is being said about Catholicism by various fundamentalists, and he provides sound responses.

_____. *The Usual Suspects: Answering Anti-Catholic Fundamentalists*. Ignatius Press, 2000. A good discussion of common arguments used by fundamentalists to criticize the Catholic Church—includes sound rebuttals.

McBrien, Richard P., *Catholicism*. Winston Press. 1980. Two volumes, but also available in a one-volume paperback *Study Edition*. A thorough review of Catholic beliefs and history; highly readable for the layperson as well as the scholar.

McKenzie, John L., *Dictionary of the Bible*. Macmillan. 1965. A comprehensive dictionary of the people, places, and beliefs in the Bible—arranged alphabetically.

Rahner, Karl and Herbert Vorgrimler, *Dictionary of Theology*. Crossroad, 1981. Somewhat technical discussions of various Catholic beliefs, arranged alphabetically; for the serious student of Catholic theology.

Swaggart, Jimmy. *Catholicism and Christianity*. Jimmy Swaggart Ministries, 1986. Rev. Swaggart provides a comprehensive fundamentalist critique of Catholic beliefs and practices.

U. S. Catholic Conference, *Catechism of the Catholic Church*. Liguori, 1995. The definitive compendium of Catholic teaching for this age.

Wcela, Emil, *The Bible: What It Is and How It Developed*. Pueblo Publishing Company, 1976. Provides essential background and explanation of biblical text. Offers individual and group reflection.

The following books and pamphlets are from Liguori Publications. These works are solid in content and highly readable.

Books

The Catechism Handbook
OSCAR LUKEFAHR, C.M.
Provides a summary of the *Catechism*'s content, explains difficult issues, and draws attention to areas of special importance.
ISBN: 978-0-8924-3864-8

Catechism of the Catholic Church
2nd Edition, Compact Catechism
Officially approved by Pope John Paul II, this is the primary source of Catholic teaching. Draws from sacred Scripture, Western and Eastern traditions of the Church, the liturgy, the teaching magisterium, Canon Law, and the lives and writings of the saints.
English—ISBN: 978-0-3854-7967-7
Spanish—ISBN: 978-0-3854-7984-4

A Catholic Guide to the Bible
OSCAR LUKEFAHR, C.M.
For each of the 73 books in the Bible, the author offers historical background information about its human writer and the literary style of the work. This book also gives a theological interpretation of selected key passages.
ISBN: 978-0-7648-0201-0

Come, Follow Me
The Commandments of Jesus
ANTHONY J. GITTINS
Encourages readers to reflect upon the words of Jesus, then deepen their commitment to the faith and to performing good works.
ISBN: 978-0-7648-1213-2

Dear Padre

Questions Catholics Ask

COMPILED BY THOMAS M. SANTA, C.SS.R.

A REDEMPTORIST PASTORAL PUBLICATION

A helpful tool for understanding the Catholic faith, presented in an easy question-and-answer format. The answers are written by various priests and are pastoral, written in plain language, and easy to understand.
ISBN: 978-0-7648-0987-3

The Essential Bible Handbook

A Guide for Catholics With Prayers and a Glossary of Key Terms

A REDEMPTORIST PASTORAL PUBLICATION

Helps readers understand the place of the Bible in Catholic Tradition, the history of how the Bible developed, biblical interpretation, and the use of the Bible in prayers.
ISBN: 978-0-7648-0836-4

The Essential Catholic Handbook

A Summary of Beliefs, Practices, and Prayers

Revised and Updated

A REDEMPTORIST PASTORAL PUBLICATION

FOREWORD BY FRANCIS CARDINAL GEORGE

An invaluable reference for those who want a topical summary of "what it means to be Catholic."
ISBN: 978-0-7648-1289-7

The Privilege of Being Catholic

OSCAR LUKEFAHR, C.M.

Uses Scripture, history, and revelation to highlight the tenets of faith that form the heart of Catholic tradition.
ISBN: 978-0-8924-3563-0

"We Believe…"

A Survey of the Catholic Faith

OSCAR LUKEFAHR, C.M.; FOREWORD BY JUSTIN CARDINAL RIGALI

Explores: The Bible As a Faith History; How Catholics Interpret the Bible; the Life and Teachings of Jesus; Church History/Tradition; and more.
ISBN: 978-0-8924-3536-4

We Worship
A Guide to the Catholic Mass
OSCAR LUKEFAHR, C.M.; FOREWORD BY REV. TIMOTHY M. DOLAN
Presents a positive view of the Mass and its significance to our lives. Explains the reason for worshiping at Mass and walks the reader through the various parts and rituals of the Mass. Includes newest revisions from the latest General Instruction of the Roman Missal.
ISBN: 978-0-7648-1212-5

Church History 101
A Concise Overview
CHRISTOPHER M. BELLITTO
This easy-to-read volume answers the basic question, "What did the Church look like in this particular period?" for four eras of Church history: early, medieval, Reformation, and modern. Chapters conclude with discussion questions, a list for further reading, a map, and timeline to locate the reader in place and time. Topics: "The Big Picture," "Church's Hierarchy," "Church in the Pews," and "What Made this Period Unique."
ISBN: 978-0-7648-1603-1

Mary 101
Tradition and Influence
Come on a journey to meet Jesus's mother, Mary. You'll understand the history and traditions of the Virgin in relation to the concerns of 21st-century Christians around the world. Chapters include essential background information, reflection questions, and suggested reading for furthering your understanding of Mary and the international scope of Marian concerns.
ISBN: 978-0-7648-1851-6

Scripture 101
An Intro to Reading the Bible
WILLIAM J. PARKER, C.SS.R.
This is the second book in Liguori's *101 Series,* and it takes the reader on a journey through the history of the Bible, including how the Bible came to be, learning how it was written, and understanding the Old and New Testaments in a Catholic approach.
ISBN: 978-0-7648-1700-7

Your Faith

A Practical Presentation of Catholic Belief

Offers a comprehensive study of Catholicism that is easy to understand. The basic truths of the faith are shown as progressive revelations of Jesus making himself present through the Church by revealing his message in the New Testament, then living in us through the sacraments.

ISBN: 978-0-7648-0988-0

Permissions and Resources

Scripture citations are taken from the *New Revised Standard Version of the Bible*, copyright 1989 by the Division of Christian Education of the National Council of the Churches of Christ in the USA. All rights reserved. Used with permission.

Excerpts from *Vatican II: Constitutions, Decrees, Declarations: A Completely Revised Translation in Inclusive Language* edited by Austin Flannery, O.P., copyright 1996, Costello Publishing Company, Inc., Northport, New York, are used by permission of the publisher, all rights reserved. No part of these excerpts may be reproduced, stored in a retrieval system, or transmitted in any form or by an means—electronic, mechanical, photocopying, recording, or otherwise, without express permission of Costello Publishing Company.

Excerpts from *Sharing the Light of Faith*, National Catechetical Directory for Catholics of the United States, copyrighted © 1979, by the United States Catholic Conference, Department of Education, Washington, DC, are used by permission of copyright owner. All rights reserved.

Excerpts from the English translation of *The Roman Missal*, copyright © 1973, International Committee on English in the Liturgy, Inc. All rights reserved.

Excerpts from the English translation of the *Catechism of the Catholic Church* for the United States of America, copyright © 1994, United States Catholic Conference, Inc.—Libreria Editrice Vaticana; English translation of the *Catechism of the Catholic Church: Modifications from the Editio Typica,* copyright © 1997, United States Catholic Conference, Inc.—Libreria Editrice Vaticana. Used with permission.

Other Related Liguori Publications Titles

Handbook for Today's Catholic
Revised Edition

Handbook for Today's Catholic is presented in easy-to-understand language, with content divided into Beliefs, Practices, Prayers, and Living the Faith, and is also fully indexed to the Catechism of the Catholic Church.

ISBN: 978-0-7648-1220-0

The Essential Catholic Handbook
A Summary of Beliefs, Practices, and Prayers Revised and Updated

This invaluable book for those who want a topical summary of "what it means to be Catholic," is now even more useful. This expanded edition includes a new Introduction, the current list of holy days of obligation observed in the United States, a new section on how to prepare for a sick call, an index, and much more.

ISBN: 978-0-7648-1289-7

Living the Ten Commandments as a Catholic Today
Compiled by: Mathew J. Kessler

Living the Ten Commandments as a Catholic Today is written to "open up" the commandments and make them understandable and relevant for our lives today. Their messages are timeless—tell the truth, respect your parents, don't commit adultery—but it's hard sometimes to put their meaning into the context of today's hectic, fast-paced world.

ISBN: 978-0-7648-1849-3